Cover photo: Master mechanic Lenny Skunberg and the author, Dick Williams, with the Williams' Super Cubs. Photo by Ilona McCarty

STOLIN' WITH A SUPER CUB:
BACKCOUNTRY FLYING ZEN AND MORE

R.K. "DICK" WILLIAMS AND E.K. "ED" WILLIAMS

Copyright © 2021 by R.K. Williams

2021 First Edition, First Printing
Williams Summit Publishers
(208) 861.1519

All rights reserved.
Printed in the United States

No portion of this book
may be reproduced in any way without
written permission from the publisher.

For additional copies of this book,
please contact Amazon.com or
the author at knealew@gmail.com.

ISBN: 9798717988483

Design by Dominique Etcheverry, bydominique.com

"The Super Cub is the safest airplane in the world; it can just barely kill you."

-Max Stanley, Northrup Test Pilot

FORWARD

PART 1

In November 1983, Jim Richmond, the owner of Cub Crafters in Yakima, Washington, started the Super Cub Pilot's Association (SCPA) with a newsletter. At its peak, the SCPA had over thirteen hundred members from all over the globe. Prior to the days of the internet, it was a wonderful place to go for Super Cub news. Jim was, and still is, at the leading edge of innovation, modifications, and maintenance for the Super Cub, both certified and experimental. The newsletter was always chock-full of important and interesting information.

Jim and I inevitably got to know each other and became good friends, and by 1985 he had persuaded me to become his safety editor. During my tenure until 1991, I wrote some forty-five editorials for the newsletter, and Jim was kind enough to grant me the rights to those editorials for future use. Now, finally, in 2021, I am ready to do something with them. As I reviewed these thirty-five-year-old writings, I was struck by the relevance of the words today, even with all the modifications and changes in technology. And now there is an entirely new generation of pilots to help educate!

These editorials were my first attempt at professional writing for pay. And, sometimes, it shows. But my saving grace was my father, E.K. "Ed" Williams. As a distinguished English professor (and student pilot who soloed and accumulated over fifty hours in the 1970s), he edited and co-wrote these editorials, and we had great fun working together on them. Not only did his input greatly enhance the writings, but I learned valuable techniques to apply in later writing. He refused any kind of ownership to the publications, giving me full credit, but now that he has passed, I can have the last say by giving him co-authorship of this effort. Thanks again, Dad.

My good friend Richard Holm beat me to the Idaho history story with the definitive *Bound for the Backcountry, Volumes I and II* (Richard H. Holm Jr., 2012, and Richard H. Holm Jr., 2015) and did a masterful job I could not have equaled. I got my anecdotal history in with *Notes From The Cockpit* (R.K. Williams, 2015), and my instructional bit with *Mountain, Canyon, and Backcountry Flying* (Hoover & Williams, 2019), now being called the new mountain flying bible. Richard Holm attempted to define the term "backcountry" and in the end finally decided to leave the notion to the reader, with some well-defined sidewalls. I will venture to say that it is related to bush and outback flying, and that all three types deal with unimproved landing sites in remote areas. Backcountry sites might tend to have higher elevations and density altitudes in general, and non-standard approaches and departures to actual airstrips. For my somewhat narrow purposes, I will generally describe "backcountry" as the remote country of the northwest United States. The bush and outback (primarily Alaska and Africa) might tend to have more off-field landing areas, with many of them at lower elevations and with more open approach paths. But these are generalities. All three are kin to each other, and the labels are not really that important. In this book, these operations are called backcountry. Aviation readers will understand the title term "STOL" (Short Take-Off and Landing aircraft).

Supercub.org, operated by Steve Johnson, basically replaced the SCPA and is one of the premier aircraft websites out there today. There is a lot of good discussion on Steve's website, but I still wanted to do something with these articles, which I considered of value to all general aviation pilots although they have not been available for several decades.

Those thoughts brought this effort to fruition, and Part I is the new edition of these editorials.

My thanks to Dr. Amy Hoover, co-author of *Mountain, Canyon, and Backcountry Flying*, for laboriously giving these words scrutiny for coherence and accuracy while dealing with a full-time job during the Covid Crisis. Her advice and assistance are always top-notch.

On Christmas day 1984 there were three Super Cub accidents in the United States. One of them was a dual fatality in Nevada involving my wife's extended family. The pilot was low-time, inexperienced, and attempting to perform a task beyond his expertise. This effort goes out to him and his family with the hope that a similar tragedy can be avoided.

PART 2

Here we discuss the rebuilding and modification (de-Piperizing) of two certified Super Cubs, one an original Agricultural (A) Model and the other which started out as an L-18C with a 90 hp Continental motor. These aircraft were both rebuilt at the turn of the century, and newer

Cubs have lighter electronic instrumentation and avionics available, even including autopilots that might make sense because of their size and weight. However, the other actual performance changes, except perhaps for elimination of the bungee gear, remain relatively minor at this point.

PART 3

Part 3 is an outline of the mental processes of high-grade backcountry flying. We delve into the thought processes and self-enlightenment that is crucial to avoid the pitfalls and dangers of bent metal or worse. It is a career-long process that never ends and is fraught with lapses, set-backs, forgetfulness, and denial, which makes it quite a roller coaster ride.

Dad/my co-author and me.

PREFACE

I flew my first Super Cub in 1976. It was a stock 1960 Cub, N3761Z, owned by the Solar Flying Club, Inc. and I flew it for seven dollars an hour wet (fuel included). My first taildragger, just prior to the Cub, was an eighty-five horsepower 1946 Aeronca Champ (Air Knocker) that cost a whopping five dollars an hour, and it was fun, but I immediately fell in love with the old Cub. I was in Grangeville, Idaho, and had mentors like Frank Hill and Bob Black who introduced me to the famous Idaho backcountry. I had some fine times cutting my teeth with lost brakes on a downhill taxi, broken rudder pedals, and yelling back to my passengers without headsets or intercoms. You can read about some of those antics in *Notes From The Cockpit* (R.K. Williams, 2015).

After a few moves around the state, I found myself in Salmon, Idaho, with my dream job as a commercial backcountry pilot. But after a couple of years, I found myself itching to find a unique aviation niche to supplement my real job.

A Super Cub seemed like the logical place to start. There was one on the field, owned by an old Alaskan bush pilot, and it even had the old Goodyear Blimp twenty-six-inch tundra tires on it. The owner, Buck Holt, was a crotchety old guy who wasn't afraid to land just about anywhere, legal or not. At that time, around 1981, I could only account for about six Super Cubs in the entire state of Idaho.

With a loan from my parents and the expertise of GAMA Maintenance Technician of the Year Lenny Skunberg, we found a 1957 A model, serial number 6627, in a farmer's hangar in Nebraska. It was stripped down stock, with no radios or shielded magneto harness, and it cost $14,000, but it was mine!

Then began the bottomless pit to put money into, as all boat and airplane owners understand. But we got it up to speed with the basics so I could start one of the first mountain flying schools in the United States, and eventually so I could become a contract pilot for the USDA predator control program.

I had found the niche! And it meshed perfectly with my air taxi job which was primarily in the summer and fall, while the predator control took place in the winter and spring. The instruction, fish and game work, and predator control quickly paid the bills and paid for the airplane, and I still could not find another working Super Cub in Idaho.

That Super Cub is still part of the family, co-owned by my son and me. As of this writing the airplane is sixty-three years old, and we have owned it for thirty-nine of those years.

INTRODUCTION

This is not a book about the J series or other PA numbered Cubs, because that history is rich and quite well documented. The SCPA editorials included other Short Take Off and Landing (STOL) aircraft (primarily the Cessna 185) and there are so many new STOL airplanes out there today, including the experimental Cubs, that there is a lot of pertinent information herein that could be valuable to all of them.

The Piper Super Cub PA-18 was first manufactured in 1949 or 1950 (published dates vary), three years after the J-3 went out of production, as an extension of the PA-11, 12, and 14. When Piper suspended production in 1982, 8364 Super Cubs had been built. Back in 2003, Canada listed 405 registered Super Cubs in their country. Today, United States Registry shows over 2000 PA18-150s, 478 PA18s, 380 PA18A-150s, and 45 PA18-150 Cub Crafter Amphibians, as well as a few other models including 13 L18Cs, which I include because my son now owns one. More on that in Part 2.

It was originally a two-place, conventional gear aircraft that cruised in the 100-mph range. New Cubs from the factory went for about $12,500 in 1953. Another source lists the Cub at $7,995 in 1955. I have been unable to verify the differences, but perhaps it was because of options. Due to the renewed interest in this type of aircraft in the last couple of decades (as well as expensive modifications), their value has increased almost a thousand percent since then. The main single modification has been the engine, starting with a 90 HP Continental, through 125, 135, 150, and now up to the Lycoming O-360 with 180 HP, or more.

TABLE OF CONTENTS

A Word on the Piper Cub ... 1

PART 1 ... 9

July 1984, Volume 2, Issue 7:
    Fly-In Report ... 11

August 1985, Volume 3, Issue 7:
    Fly-in Report #2 ... 15

March 1985, Volume 3, Issue 3:
    Letters to the Editor ... 19

December 1985, Volume 3, Issue 11:
    My Introduction ... 23

January 1986, Volume 4, Issue 1:
    More Winter Watches: When the Going
    Gets Soft…Keep Your Head Up! ... 25

February 1986, Volume 4, Issue 2:
    Winter Watches ... 29

March 1986, Volume 4, Issue 3:
    Engine Failure at Selway Lodge ... 33

May 1986, Volume 4, Issue 5:
    Hand Propping ... 37

June 1986, Volume 4, Issue 6:
    Civilian Wings ... 41

July/August 1986, Volume 4, Issue 7:
    Wait & Balance ... 45

September 1986, Volume 4, Issue 8:
    Part II Wait & Balance ... 51

October/November 1986, Volume 4, Issue 9:
  Survival 55
December 1986, Volume 4, Issue 10:
  Survival Part II 59
January 1987, Volume 5, Issue 1:
  Rehearsals and Realities 65
February 1987, Volume 5, Issue 2:
  Off-Field Operations 69
March 1987, Volume 5, Issue 3:
  Riding with Lady Luck 73
April 1987, Volume 5, Issue 4:
  Peaceful Uses of Flaps 81
May 1987, Volume 5, Issue 5:
  Springtime Brush-Up 89
June 1987, Volume 5, Issue 6:
  Checklists and Numbers 93
July 1987, Volume 5, Issue 7:
  Vital Statistics 99
August 1987, Volume 5, Issue 8:
  Power Curves 105
September 1987, Volume 5, Issue 9:
  Give Yourself a Brake 109
October 1987, Volume 5, Issue 10:
  Three Shots at the Wind 113
November 1987, Volume 5, Issue 11:
  The Wind Doesn't Blow, It Sucks 119
December 1987, Volume 5, Issue 12:
  Night Flight 123

January 1988, Volume 6, Issue 1:
    Schussing Part I 129

February 1988, Volume 6, Issue 2:
    Schussing Part II 135

Spring 1988, Volume 6, Issue 3:
    Microbursts 141

Summer 1988, Volume 6, Issue 4:
    Aircraft Language 145

Fall 1988, Volume 6, Issue 5:
    Flight Plans and Compasses 151

Winter 1988, Volume 6, Issue 6:
    Safety By the Numbers 155

Spring 1989, Volume 7, Issue 1:
    Accident Probabilities 159

Summer 1989, Volume 7, Issue 2:
    Two Versus Three, Slip Versus Crab 165

Fall 1989, Volume 7, Issue 3:
    Weather Flying 171

Winter 1989, Volume 7, Issue 4:
    On Weathering Weather 177

Spring 1990, Volume 8, Issue 1:
    Attitude Adjustment 181

Summer 1990, Volume 8, Issue 2:
    Judgment Day 187

Fall 1990, Volume 8, Issue 3:
    Decision Making and Stress 191

Winter 1990, Volume 8, Issue 4:
    Not-So-Merry Go-Arounds 195

Spring 1991, Volume 9, Issue 1:
    Twist and Shout 201
Summer 1991, Volume 9, Issue 2:
    Time and Money 205
Fall 1991, Volume 9, Issue 3:
    Stall Speeds 209
Winter 1991, Volume 9, Issue 4:
    FARs and Wingtip Vortices 215
Spring 1992, Volume 10, Issue 1:
    Adieu 217
Why I Want to Be a Pilot 219

PART 2 221

Rebuilding and Modifying a Super Cub
    at the Turn of the Century 227
Some Interesting Cub Specifciations 231
The Rebuild Story 235
N2703W 245

PART 3
Zen and the Art of Backcountry Flying 251

PHOTO GALLERY 271

INDEX 287

STOLIN' WITH A SUPER CUB

A WORD ON THE PIPER CUB

It is interesting to note that the brochure lists the Service Ceiling as 19,000', and the Absolute Ceiling as 21,300'. It would require an IFR clearance to obtain either of those altitudes. In the November 1986 issue of *Private Pilot Magazine,* Robert S. Grant wrote in his article "Piper's Perfect Rice Picker!" that Caro Bayley flew a Super Cub to 30,203' in January 1951. That airplane had to be well below gross and in colder than standard air! But Don Sheldon landed his Super Cub on Denali at over 17,000'. If you don't know about the legendary Alaskan pilot from Talkeetna, get a copy of *Wager With the Wind* (James Greiner, 1982). He was probably the primary mountain climbing air support of his day.

As for over-gross weight operations, Grant claims to have seen a Super Cub in Fort Nelson, B.C. unload five grown men and a mechanic's toolbox! It is undoubtedly an aircraft famous for its ability to haul heavy loads, but that sounds like a Volkswagen Bug college prank to me. No thanks!

Clarence and Gordon Taylor of Taylorcraft Aircraft designed the original Cub in 1930, but it didn't have a name. William T. Piper acquired Taylor Aircraft, but he wasn't a pilot and knew next to nothing about the airplane business. When Taylor's new aircraft made its first brief flight, Piper's accountant noted that it was powered by a 20 horsepower Brownback Tiger Kitten engine and made a momentous suggestion: "Why not call the plane the Cub?" Cub it became.

Although the Cub is famous for being easy to fly, the quote often attributed to Northrup test pilot Max Stanley is just as famous: "The Cub is the safest airplane built. It can just barely kill you." (Pinterest.com, 2013).

Cubs have always been judged more on where they could go than on how fast they could get there. If you want to go fast, don't fly a Cub.

And the Cub has survived in combat. Allegedly a Cub was the first American aircraft fired upon at Pearl Harbor. A Honolulu attorney out for an early morning hop over Diamond Head had his yellow Cub riddled with bullets by the first wave of Japanese fighters (Bill Cox, Piper Owner Society).

When Richard Holm was writing "Bound For the Backcountry, Volume II," he asked me to write an insert about the Super Cub, since it was such a large part of the development of Hells Canyon on the Idaho border.

A Word on the Piper Cub

When talking about backcountry planes, several classics come to mind: De Havilland Beavers and Otters, Ford Tri-Motors, Travel Air 6000s, Cessna 185s and 206s, and maybe a Britten-Norman Islander. But perhaps the most classic of all in the Hells Canyon country of Oregon and Idaho, if not the most venerable, is the trusty Piper Cub. First designed in the 1930s with the J-series, it had a light frame covered with fabric, a two-seat tandem configuration, and engines ranging from forty-five to eighty-five horsepower. They were relatively cheap and utile, with slow stall speeds that allowed pasture and other short-field operations.

After World War II the Js were followed by the

PA-series. The marquee of this model was introduced in 1949 and designated as the Super Cub. It was essentially a grown-up J-3, a little beefier all around, with of course more power (135 hp motor). The Super Cub has had an integral history with any bush or backcountry operation, but they became the principal pair of wings commercial operators and ranchers used on the short rocky landing patches of the middle Snake River region. The Super Cub was indeed the backbone of aviation in that area, for often the airstrips were never improved beyond the potential of a Super Cub. Their short-field capabilities were unmatched, making them the first choice of pilots everywhere when a new field was to be tested, whether it was on a steep mountainside or a river gravel bar. Every early backcountry pilot has flown a Cub at some time or another.

However, these early Cubs were vastly different than the highly modified versions seen winging their way through the canyon today. A portion of the stock Cub's success can be attributed to the pilot's skills and abilities. The Cubs of the middle Snake River pioneer flying days generally sported stock tires, brakes, power plants, propellers, wings, etc. But perhaps, the very essence of the plane is that it lends itself to extensive modifications, which makes it unique. Comparatively, other classic backcountry machines have seen very few modifications, except for larger engines and turbo-chargers. The Cub, on the other hand, has been "de-Piperized" to the extreme. The engines now often develop 180 to over 200 horsepower. They throw large "Borer" type propellers (Roger Borer was the holder of an STC that swapped the wimpy Sensenich stock propeller to a longer, beefier McCauley model). One popular mod even changes the thrust angle of the motor by changing the firewall attachment! The landing gear can be beefed up, with safety cables to help hold it in place if the landing area is so unimproved things break. Oversized low pressure "tundra" or "bush" tires enable the little plane to roll over holes or rocks of a substantial size that would break standard size tires and wheels. The puny diaphragm style brakes can even be replaced with high-pressure disc brakes. The original configuration of the joystick located in the right, throttle in the left, and challenging heel brakes has mostly stayed true. Conversions to toe brakes are often considered "poor form" by Cub purists.

Safety alterations, such as wing strut reinforcements, cross braces over the pilot's head, header-less fuel systems, and inertial reel shoulder harnesses, are also popular.

And of course, the interior of the aircraft has been modified to carry more gear, and sometimes allow even some creature comforts! A few hard-core Cub owners strip them down like a racing car, with virtually no interior, electrical, or starting equipment. They might weigh less than a thousand pounds empty with a minimum of 180 horsepower. The result is an impressive power to weight ratio! The revered Cub wing, however, has actually seen little improvement with the exception of vortex generators. The wing has been played with a lot including extensions, longer flaps, longer ailerons, cuffed leading edges, and wingtips. But many pilots, when all is said and done, prefer little to no mods to the wings.

Make no mistake. These highly modified Super Cubs of today are nothing like the Super Cubs involved in the aviation history of Hells Canyon. What the pioneers did with their little stock machines is remarkable (Richard H. Holm, Jr., 2015).

I would venture to say that today a factory stock Super Cub is a rarer item than a highly modified one. In Part 2 we will discuss modifications at length. Ingenious people have taken a classic airplane and made it great, starting with people like Rodger Borer, Atley Dodge, and Jim Richmond back in the previous century.

Rodger Borer was an Alaskan aviation pioneer who was born in 1922 and died in 2004. He was nicknamed the "Lone Ranger" for his independent style and development of many STCs for refinements and modifications to Super Cubs. One of his most famous, the Borer Prop, is still popular today.

F. Atlee Dodge was another Alaskan who was inducted into the Alaska Aviation Hall of Fame. He was born in 1922 and died in 2010. In the 1960s he started a business specializing in the Super Cub. He eventually sold the business to Univair in the mid 1980s. He also held dozens of STCs for the Super Cub and was known as "Mr. Super Cub". I had the pleasure of meeting Mr. Dodge in the 1990s, but I could see that his reputation as "Mr. Grouch" was only skin deep.

PART 1

***

SCPA SAFETY EDITORIALS

The Fly-Ins

The SCPA began Cub fly-ins in 1984. By then Jim Richmond and I were acquainted and I helped with some of the planning, recommending Chamberlain Basin (U79) as one of the easier airstrips to act as base camp for the Idaho wilderness. Afterwards Jim honored me with a plaque declaring me "Best Super Cub Pilot" although I did little to earn it. The second fly-in was held at the Root Ranch, close to Chamberlain, and the third was combined with the first annual Sentimental Journey to Lock Haven, Pennsylvania, for all fabric-covered Piper aircraft. Then the 1987 Journey commemorated the 50th anniversary of the J-3, the famous yellow Piper first certificated in 1937. Here are Jim's notes on the first two Super Cub Fly-Ins.

July 1984, Volume 2, Issue 7
Fly-In Report

The First Annual Super Cub Pilot's Association Fly-In is History! We had a great time, with 30 Super Cubs and 5 or 6 lesser airplanes, we filled both sides of the Chamberlain, Idaho airstrip and camped "under the wing" for a couple of days. The 21 planes that arrived late Friday afternoon were greeted with gusty winds of near 30 mph. After some scouting around, we determined the west end of the airport was the best campsite, so most Cubbers migrated to the shelter of the trees there. Later, in the afternoon, the wind went down and did not return for the rest of the weekend. The sky was blue and the temperature was probably in the low 80s.

Our campsite was surrounded by deer and elk, with spottings in the hundreds, as well as a few moose! There was one lazy old moose that spent the weekend in a pond just off the end of the runway we were using! (Sunbathing?) I was expecting to see a lot of wildlife, but I didn't expect moose!

Saturday was the official start of the Fly-In. We started with a short take-off contest. We had all types of Super Cubs from a 90 HP to the 150s with STOL kits and all the bells and whistles. Our 5700' elevation and very warm temperature stretched the take-off rolls to well over 400 feet for most contestants. Mike Combs, from Shady Cove, Oregon, won the contest in his very light PA18-135. Your official secretary, (me), somehow lost the little yellow paper that recorded Mike's takeoff distance, but if memory serves me, it was around the 360' mark. Upon landing, we were supposed to see who could come closest to the "spot" by landing 3-point and staying 3-point (i.e. no bounces). Of all the hot shot, super ace, A#1 Super Cub Jockeys there, not one managed to even qualify for the spot landing event! Everyone either bounced out of the 50' "in-bounds" area or missed it entirely. In all fairness, there was a 5-mph tailwind, and a downward slope in our landing area, so it wasn't easy to stay on the ground without bouncing. In fact, I think everyone there would agree that it was impossible!

The next event was flour bombing with a short field landing. The rules for flour bombing were simple: stay above the tree tops and hit the bulls-eye. Most of the bombs that landed in Idaho were 20' or further from the mark, except one lonesome bag of flour that hit 14" off the spot. Mike Combs strikes again!

Short field landing rules required the pilot to touch down with the main wheels beyond a specified chalk line, stop, and be measured. The tail wheel could touch before the chalk line, but not the mains. I somehow got stopped in 210' to take the trophy, but some people say I cheated by driving up to the line on my tailwheel, then chopping power and dumping flaps to let the mains drop over the line. You don't believe I would do something like that do you? (The same people wouldn't let me compete in the short take off contest because I had a cylinder of helium in the back seat.)

The last event of the day was the balloon popping contest, followed by a re-run of the spot landing contest—only this time "the spot" was uphill and into the wind, and we enlarged the boundaries to 100'. To pop a balloon, the pilot took off, made a 180 turn and positioned himself over a certain place (about a mile away) at 200' AGL. Two helium-filled balloons were released at this point, and all he had to do was drive his big propeller into the poor little balloons and pop them. Simple, right? Of all the balloons we released, all but two of them may be in orbit still. Sarge Hoem, of Dillon, Montana, and Steve Hulstrand of Roll, Arizona, tied with one pop each. Steve also won the spot landing contest upon landing with a near perfect touch down.

Sunday morning found us bound for breakfast at a nearby lodge. We then followed Dick Williams of Salmon, Idaho in his Super Cub on a tour of several of the strips in the area. We ended up at the Flying B Ranch for an excellent lunch.

It was a great time. Lots of new friendships were begun, tires were kicked, yarns were spun around campfires, etc. The company was great. Everyone had an interesting story to tell, or a question to find an answer for. I've received a lot of encouraging words about the Fly-In. all of them seem to say "let's do it again next year!" We will!

August 1985, Volume 3, Issue 7

One of the things that kept me busy in July was the Second Annual Super Cub Fly-In. My wife and I headed east July 4th to find the Root Ranch snuggled in among towering mountains of the Idaho Rockies in the Idaho Wilderness Area. We landed in the early afternoon at the 5000' high sod strip beside a beautiful log lodge and rustic cabins. The wind sock did a 360 as we were on final approach and after the 3rd or 4th bounce I felt my wife's grip on the back of my seat and a worried "Are we alright??" from the back seat. We learned later that this strip isn't usually used after 10 a.m. in the morning until 5 or 6 in the evening because of the tricky summer winds. Those winds plagued us the rest of the weekend.

Cubs began arriving from all over the states. From Texas to Nebraska, North Dakota to Arizona, Super Cubs found their way to the tall mountains of central Idaho and our 1900' of level sod. Kerry Hedge won honors as the farthest from home with his trek from New Iberia, Louisiana. He had just finished completely rebuilding and recovering his Super Cub, complete with wheel pants. He made the 25-hour flight with no problems. By Friday night, 70 to 80 people were spinning yarns about flights gone by and getting acquainted in the big log lodge.

A deer looked in on us at breakfast Saturday morning, not 20 feet away from the chow hall door. On Sunday I got to watch a young moose under the wing of someone's Cub for a half hour. The Idaho Wilderness Area is completely free of such modern amenities as roads, telephones or vehicles of any kind…except boats and airplanes.

Alex Newman arrived at the Fly-In a few days early with a Yamaha 70 growing over the side of his otherwise slick bird's fuselage. When he taxied past a Forest Ranger at Chamberlain, the ranger jumped the airport fence full stride to catch up with Alex and warn him of the penalties involved if the wheels of that "motorized vehicle" should happen to touch the ground in the Wilderness Area! It's refreshing to see how well modern man can survive without these "essentials." Backpackers, white water rafters and hunters keep a squadron of airplanes and numerous lodges busy during the summer and fall months. It's a Super Cub Heaven.

Saturday started off with a poker run. Each pilot navigated to five different airports to pick a card from the deck that had been left at the foot of the wind socks the previous day. We all arrived at Johnson Creek (5000' high and 4000' long) about mid-morning with cards in hand. Bob "Poker Face" Woodhouse, from Roll, Arizona, took top honors with hand amid jeers of "misdeal" and "re-shuffle." All was in fun though and we lined our Cubs up nose to tail for the short field take-off and short field landing contest. About the time we all converged on Johnson Creek, the Cessna 180/185 Club also landed and set up camp. There were ten or twelve 180s and 185s lining the side of the field, so we had plenty of spectators to critique our take-offs and landings. We made it clear from the very beginning that the big Cessna's were welcome to complete. Alas…no takers.

I didn't look at the thermometer, but I am sure the temperature was into the 80s as we took our turns at the short field take-off, a trip around to final, and a short field landing, then park at the end of the line. I went around first and got off in 172'7" and bounced to a halt in 266'7". That take-off distance proved to be shortest. Vaughn Johnson of Bozeman, Montana got off in 189 feet and Steve Pankonin of Shady Cove, Oregon was airborne in 195 feet. The shortest landing was 172 feet by Steve Pankonin again, and Bob "Poker Face" Woodhouse stopped in 216 for second place. Vaughn Johnson took third place with 225 feet. All was in fun and spectators and pilots alike had something to hash over as the wind came up and put a stop to our flying. It was lunch time anyway and the good folks at the Root Ranch had packed a delicious fried chicken picnic lunch.

The wind didn't stop after lunch as I had planned, and we waited, and waited and WAITED for the gusts to stop. Supper time came and went. A few of us borrowed an old truck and drove five miles to town for some pop and gas. We finally headed back to the "Root" for a late supper around 7. A long afternoon for me, as I wanted to stay on schedule, but no one else seemed to mind.

We awarded trophies and ribbons Saturday evening and had a good time until the wee hours of the morning. Sunday after breakfast some said goodbye and headed home, a group flew over the hill to another fly-in air show at McCall, and the rest headed down the river to the Flying "B" for lunch. I flew a load of gear out to Salmon and called home to check on the little ones, and found that our babysitter had gotten quite sick, so Sue and I beat feet home as fast as our little bird could carry us.

We learned some important lessons about planning

and organizing events such as this, and next year hope that we will be able to have an even better fly-in for all to enjoy.

I was becoming more and more involved with the SCPA and had eventually written the following short letter out of safety concerns.

March 1985, Volume 3, Issue 3

Dear Editor,

I have read with much interest all the information in the newsletter regarding coyote hunting. Without putting too much of a damper on the fun and enthusiasm, I would like to point out some sobering facts in the interest of safety.

First, check your insurance for coyote hunting. Avemco, for one, will not cover your aircraft during any hunting, private or commercial. Second, the skill level necessary for low level predator control is extremely high. It is just about the toughest flying I do, and I am a high time professional with a lot of low level experience. Trying to maneuver around a moving object on the ground, while getting as close as possible to that object, is a real invitation to uncoordinated slow flight. It is difficult to do! Let us also consider the aircraft we are flying. Fantastic airplane that the Super Cub is (and we all love it!), the airfoil does have a fairly vicious stall/spin characteristic. With full power and some flaps (a typical configuration for a turn during hunting), the Cub will snap over into a spin very quickly if it stalls with the rudder out of trim. I urge all pilots doing this kind of flying to get and stay current in stall/spin training with a good instructor. Know what to avoid, because if you stall/spin during coyote hunting, you will not have enough time to recover!

Sincerely,
Dick Williams

And before that, in March 1984:

Greetings! I hope this letter finds you recovering from the long winter and anticipating the long summer. It seems easier for me to sit down in the middle of the winter and write about flying my Super Cub than it is now in the spring. In winter, I fight cold engines, cold cockpits, even cold earphones and stick grips to go out and fly a little while. I'd almost rather sit down by the fire with a hot cup of tea and fantasize about what I'll do next spring, how I'll fly into this strip or that one. It's easier to sit and dream about it than it is to go out into the cold and wind and do it. But…

Now the warm days are returning, the sun is shining and my mind is not off in Super Cub Fantasy Land, it's outside in the sunshine! Ah, that little bend in the river would make a good place to land, plenty of room, good gravel…good approach…green grass off the side…

Boy, with that high-quality writing, I'm surprised I ended up as a regular columnist for Jim! And what a wuss! Whining about flying in a little cold? Not too many years later I would find myself hunting coyotes in Oregon at -30º Fahrenheit!

Later that year, I wrote another letter, doing some blatant advertising:

Dear Jim:

I think the CUB Association is a great idea! I'm the chief pilot with Salmon Air Taxi in Salmon, Idaho. We specialize in flying the Idaho back country. I lease my own Super Cub to the company, and we do everything from coyote control to Fish & Game fish counts to instruction through our Mountain Flying School.

My Cub is a 1957 A model with 2000 hours total time, recovered in 1980. Some of the features include a PA-25 tail spring with 2 hole 3200 Scott tailwheel (this set up will not break in the backcountry!), beefed up main gear (steel axle inserts) with Cleveland brakes, 8:50 x 6" wheels and brakes, extended baggage, metal belly and headliner, removable back seat cross bar, back stick cover, Borer prop, 3 notch flaps, 20 mph airspeed indicator, gear safety cables, leading edge tape on the gear V's, struts, and stabilizer (this prevents a lot of gravel nicks), and a Sigtronics intercom with David Clark headsets (a necessity to retain legal hearing). Further mods planned include the 60-gallon fuel tanks, defroster and heat robber kits, fuel steps, a vertical card compass, a tow hook, seaplane door on the left, and a larger more comfortable front seat. We call this "De-Piperizing" the Cub.

My maintenance is done by Lenny's Airmotive here in Salmon. He's a super mechanic who also does all of the company maintenance.

The Borer prop took a little getting used to, but

it does improve performance, mostly in the slow flight range. I also like the 20, 37, and 50-degree flap settings, especially for low-level game counts.

Now for questions: What can I find out about a good comfortable front seat replacement? Also, I'm curious how much beefier the A model is, and where that strength has been added. Also, Jim, what do you know about these "seaplane" or "coyote" left swing windows and doors?

Also, if I can do a little advertising, anyone interested in some of the best mountain and canyon flying in the world, and a mountain flying school qualified to teach in it, call Salmon Air Taxi. We are one of the very few FAA approved mountain flying schools in the nation, and we offer basic, advanced, and custom-tailored courses.

If I'm correct it was you who stopped in Salmon on your way to Gillette the other day. Sorry I missed you. Next time any of you Cub pilots are in the area, stop and say hi. Salmon's a great little place and I can give you tips on some nice Cub-camping strips nearby.

Sincerely,
Dick Williams
Salmon, Idaho

Well, it is easy to see that was back in the beginning days of Super Cub modifications, many moons ago. Some of those mods were replaced with better mods, and some were fantasies that never materialized. More about that in Part 2.

In conversations with Jim, he had told me the NTSB had sent him Super Cub accidents from a two-year period that amounted to one accident a week, with only one being related to engine failure.

We began talking about Super Cub Safety. Here was my introduction by Jim:

December 1985, Volume 3, Issue 11
Dick Williams—Safety Editor

Those of you who have come to the SCPA Fly-Ins in the Idaho Wilderness have met Dick Williams. Dick has been the Chief Pilot for Salmon Air Taxi for the last several years and has earned a reputation as one of the "back-country's" most reliable and professional pilots. He's flown over 6000 hours in Idaho's backcountry, where the wind and weather change with the hands on a clock, and distances are covered only by pack horses, jet boats, and airplanes. A Super Cub owner and pilot, Dick took his first airplane ride in a Cub at age 15. He's got a lot of experience by now in both the front and back seat of a Cub.

Dick wrote the ground school curriculum for Salmon Air Taxi's Mountain Flying School and has been awarded the State of Idaho's 11 Year Safe Pilot Award, in addition to being named an FAA Accident Prevention Counselor in 1984. He's flown his Cub 300 hours for the Department of Agriculture, chasing coyotes, and has varied experience in most areas of flying that we Super Cub Pilot's find ourselves in.

As Safety Editor, Dick will have the responsibility of keeping us reminded of the laws of aerodynamics as they relate to a Super Cub, and of bringing to mind areas that we might be getting a little rusty in. He may touch on some things that we don't want to hear.

Dick is married, with two children, and lives in a log home just off the end of Salmon's main runway. He'll be adding a great deal to our newsletter, and I, for one, welcome him aboard.

–Jim Richmond, Editor

And so it started. Since it was winter time, soft field operations and ski flying seemed apropos.

January 1986, Volume 4, Issue 1
More Winter Watches
When the Going Gets Soft.... Keep Your Head Up!

The pilot of a recently restored Cub was describing the way he had tipped over during a takeoff attempt from the Cold Meadows airstrip in the Idaho Mountains. The strip had about eight inches of snow (my limit is normally six inches for wheels). Still not quite believing what had happened, he said, "It was just about ready to fly! I had the tail up…" Poor guy. His tail might have been ready to fly, but his head sure wasn't. You could call him the victim of typical primary training, in which most pilots do not have real experiences with soft fields; they and their instructors do a few practice landings and takeoffs under simulated or imagined conditions. In a real, unexpected situation, instinct can produce exactly the wrong response. And in this pilot's case, it did.

North country pilots don't have to be reminded that winter landing strips get layered with snow, ice, slush, and mud. And it pays to keep sharp on soft field techniques—a few reminders can help keep your Cub's nose clean. (You lucky pilots headed down to the beaches of Mexico for the winter—you could run into some strips that are too soft for comfort, too).

In one of my first critical soft field episodes, in a Cessna 185, I was saved by a combination of luck, coyote tracks, and remembered training. It was early spring, and a new boss was on board, headed for Boise to pick up some Forest Service people. The weather was rotten, and before becoming completely boxed in I elected to land at Indian Creek on the Middle Fork of the Salmon River.

The snow was only about four inches deep but very wet and heavy. A coyote ran across the field as we were on short final—I remember looking at and thinking about his mushy tracks. As soon as I touched down, in a good three-point landing with some power, the tail began to rise. (Believe me, the natural reaction in that situation is to hit the brakes and bring the power off). I fought off the natural reaction, pulled the yoke back into my lap, and added **full power.** The tail slowly—ever so slowly—came back down. But it took full power to taxi. The power blast kept the tail down.

Then we had the fun of spending most of the day shoveling a track to take off in. We got home just before dark. The soft field takeoff, with my feet dancing on those rudders, the yoke right in my lap, and our eyes wide open, was "uneventful" (The tail stayed down).

The Idaho back country seems to eat at least one airplane every year in soft field conditions. At the SCPA Fly-In last summer you may have seen the tail section of a 182 in the trees at the Root Ranch. That decoration was the result of poor technique in the bog that so often develops there. There is a long, interesting, and somewhat terrifying story about three airplanes nosing over in one episode at Cold Meadows which is 7030' high. Mostly, those accidents happen when the mud or snow is simply too deep for safe operations.

Sometimes no amount of skill and quick reaction will save you. But your chances are far better if you remember the special techniques and practice them: land and take off in a three-point attitude with plenty of power. Use extreme caution in deciding to start the procedure. Don't trust layman's reports; insist on the word from a pilot, and if you are in doubt, if it doesn't feel good—don't do it.

On that takeoff, staying in the narrow-shoveled tracks was critical. If I had wandered out into the un-shoveled muck, I would have certainly had my hands full. I certainly didn't impress my new boss on that flight. Ski flying has gotten more popular these days, and "Mountain, Canyon, and Backcountry Flying" (Hoover and Williams, 2019) has a good chapter on those operations. Big tires have also become popular, but don't think they can replace skis! Their large frontal area can break through crust and become an instant brake and cause a nose-over.

February 1986, Volume 4, Issue 2
Winter Watches

In mid-winter, landing on some surfaces can be about as comfortable as stepping over a sleeping mother grizzly. A few years ago, on a Fish & Game charter flight to the Flying B Ranch on the Middle Fork of the Salmon River, the field actually rose up and swatted me. On the strip, about three inches of fresh powder lay on top of eight inches of hard packed snow, which made it landable with wheels. The ranch foreman had been feeding the horses on the runway—tooling a jeep up and down, tossing cut hay with a pitchfork. What I didn't know was that the pitchfork had mysteriously disappeared a couple of days earlier, and that my left main tire would relocate it. I was still wondering about a sudden loud pop (my tire blowing) when the wooden end of the fork jumped up into the prop (luckily for me, only the wood hit the plane, leaving the prop in much better shape than the pitchfork handle). About two hours later we finished the tire repair and got back home just before dark. If we hadn't been at a civilized place—i.e. one with adequate tools-we would have had to consider hibernation as a solution to our problem. Sometimes, no matter how careful pilots are, incidents like that are unavoidable, and remind us of the wisdom of carrying complete survival gear.

On the subject of winter hazards, oil breather tubes are high on the list. Do you know the location of that tube? If the end is out in the slipstream or anywhere where the opening at the end can freeze, pressure can build up in the crankcase, blow your engine seals, and completely dump your engine oil. One remedy is to put an additional hole in the breather tube, three or four inches up from the bottom. Another is to shorten the tube. Check with your mechanic; he would probably rather fix a breather tube than replace an engine.

Carb Ice

I also ask you to think about carb ice, and it's dangerous, hard-to-predict behavior. In the throat of the carburetor, where fuel and air are mixed, the air temperature is lowered about thirty-eight degrees as vaporization and evaporation take place; therefore, and OAT of 70 degrees is ideal for icing conditions: 70-38=32. All you need is moisture for ice to form. Carb heat is a must.

In very cold temperatures, however, the application of carb heat can actually create icing conditions by warming the air to critical icing ranges. Ice is most likely to form between 0 degrees and 32 degrees F. carb intake temperature, which is 32 to 70 degrees OAT. Carb heat warms the intake about thirty degrees. If OAT is -20°F, carb heat will raise the carb intake temperature to a hazardous 10 degrees F.

Another vital consideration is that carb heat enrichens the mixture. In an emergency we are taught to apply carb heat immediately, and many pilots also richen the mixture. Actually, it should be leaned, if anything, as you apply carb heat; otherwise, you may flood the engine and cause it to quit. (My commercial flight examiner loved to catch applicants on that one-one of his pet questions. My instructor, having the inside scoop, warned me in advance. Lucky again).

Fortunately, or unfortunately, luck and our attitudes about luck play a key part in aviation. I'll talk more about that, along with knowledge and experience, next month.

Total engine failure on a short mountain airstrip is not anything to look forward to. I had some luck, and maybe some interesting intuition, on this unforgettable episode

March 1986 Volume 4, Issue 3
Engine Failure at Selway Lodge

One of the thrills of flying you can do without is having your engine cut out during takeoff. But it's not the engine's fault if your head and hand are telling it to run and your elbow has told it to stop.

Picture yourself at a marginal airstrip on the Selway River, in the Idaho Selway-Bitterroot Wilderness Area. It is late fall—hunting season is over, but there is one last elk to fly out. The hunters and lodge owners have left, and no one is around for miles. You land in poor weather, on five inches of snow. You load up the elk and evaluate the takeoff.

Because, eight years before, the lodge owner planted grass on the hill at the end of the strip, you are not supposed to use that hill for takeoff. But no one is around, you figure that the grass is dormant and well-padded anyway, and you elect to taxi up the hill for a good takeoff run. As you begin to roll, you see that the forward trim needs your expert touch. You reach down to rotate the trim handle forward. You do this just as you are getting airborne, and immediately the engine quits. Dead. Luckily, you have enough runway left to land on "un-eventfully." If you hadn't used the hill, however, you wouldn't have had either runway or a safe alternative. You decide, among other things, that you will replant grass on your hands and knees, if necessary; but you will continue to use the hill on occasion.

Next, you very seriously review your piloting skills. I know, because the story I told really happened to me one cold, late November. On the way back up the hill (making a second track in the grass) I thought about the culprit, the toggle-type mag switches located above the trim handle in my Cub. I was aware that a service letter had circulated regarding those switches, and I had had safety shields installed on them, but my bulky coat had still managed to knock both toggles down to the off position. Within two days my friendly mechanic had installed the preferred key type mag switch on the panel. If your Cub has toggle mag switches located above the trim handle, please don't wait to demonstrate, as I did, that they are unsafe.

My compliments to Jeff Green for his useful article on glide speeds. The Cub operating manual coverage on this point is sketchy, and Green's computerized information is interesting, surprising and valuable in understanding how headwinds and tailwinds affect gliding speeds. Readers, I recommend you taking a moment to clip this information from page 5 of the December newsletter and pasting it in the back of your Cub manual, with thanks to Green. I hear that he will be sending in more information soon on Cubs on wheels.

Last month's editorial mentioned the elements of skill and luck in aviation. In my Mountain Flying Course, the elements of flying are divided into skills, knowledge and judgment, because that division is useful for instruction and for any pilot's self-assessment. Future issues will make use of those categories in sorting out some general problems of piloting as well as some special problems of mountain flying. Cards and letters welcome!

This was only one of several adventures I experienced at Selway Lodge. You can read more in "Notes From The Cockpit" (R.K. Williams, 2015). It's a beautiful, private place with some potential gotchas.

May 1986, Volume 4, Issue 5
Hand Propping

In spring, when most of the world is bouncing to life, airplane batteries tend to be like me after a long winter: slow, out of shape, and weak. At some airstrips, a low battery leaves you with four options—jump start, new battery, hand prop, or walking. If the first two aren't feasible or available, you're down to either hand propping or footwork.

Statistics show that many pilots have made the wrong decision. They should have walked. Hand propping accidents are numerous, often maiming or deadly. Therefore, common advice from instructors about hand propping is, "Don't!" Hand propping skills seem to have gone the way of radial engines, uncontrolled airspace and tailwheels.

But the need for those skills continues to exist. The average single engine pilot, including the Super Cub pilot, is eventually likely to be in an isolated spot with a dead battery. And **before** that happens, I urge you to find a competent, **experienced** instructor for twenty minutes of dual in prop-starting your airplane. It may take some time to find someone competent. In the meanwhile, I will mention a few important points, if only to emphasize that written instruction is no substitute for hands on teaching and practice.

First of all, it's dangerous. That's right—dangerous. There is definitely a higher level of risk than turning a key or pushing a button. But, properly done, it is a calculated risk with few physical hazards. And it is part of aviation,

especially mountain flying.
1. Secure the airplane with brakes, tie-downs (tail particularly), and chocks.
2. Have solid footing for yourself in front of the prop.
3. Double check throttle, mixture, and mag settings (do not use assistants in the cockpit unless they are trained and familiar with your aircraft).
4. After the prop is at TDC (top dead center) and you are ready to start, barely crack the throttle open and turn on the left mag (the only one with an impulse coupling). Various cold or hot start procedures exist; learn the proper ones for your aircraft.
5. Footing under the prop is critical. You naturally tend to stand back; but you're actually safer with your feet up close. It is hazardous if your upper body is off balance and leaning into the prop. As you pull the prop through to TDC, always expect a hot mag; be in position to get away from the prop. When you have the prop in place for a pull, just before you begin, swing your left leg forward, so it's coming back as you pull. This leg action will help develop momentum back away from the prop.
6. If the engine starts, be extremely prudent as you walk around, loading and untying your airplane. If the engine doesn't start, please turn off your mag before rotating the prop to TDC. If someone is helping you in the cockpit, use a clear set of signals to verify that your assistant has set everything—

brakes, mixture, throttle, and mags—exactly the way you want.

7. Details vary. The use of gloves is debatable. (I would use them myself on a sharp blade). Don't wear rings or bracelets. Don't curl your fingers around the blade. And on the J3s and floatplanes, many pilots prefer to stand behind the prop, in front of the strut, on the right side, where they can reach everything and be behind the prop.

In the Idaho Wilderness there is an isolated, intimidating, roly-poly airstrip called Soldier Bar. Several years ago, I landed a 185 there to pick up two backpackers. A sluggish start in Boise that morning should have warned me about a low battery—the ammeter would have told a story, too, had I read it more attentively, and heeded the faint odor of fried rubber, which often indicates a burned alternator belt. But after arriving at Soldier Bar I unthinkingly shut down the engine. After loading and attempting to start up, I realized we had a problem.

Now, a hot, fuel-injected, 300 horsepower engine is not easy to hand prop, but I was experienced and saw little option but to try, taking all precautions. Several starts made it obvious that I couldn't run around to the cockpit and hit the electric boost pumps quickly enough to keep the engine going. At that point one of the backpackers said, "Hey, I used to fly a lot with my uncle. I can help you if you want." I evaluated him, his offer, and my predicament, and decided to check him out thoroughly in the cockpit.

We commenced the propping procedure, complete with oral commands and responses between us. Somehow, just once—even after repeating the command—my assistant forgot to go "mags cold." I was pulling the prop through to TDC, carefully standing sideways to the prop, right arm bringing it down from vertical. The engine suddenly fired and started. I was in the perfect position to bring my arm down and away, along with the rest of my body. But not quite quickly enough to escape the other prop blade. As I was rolling away, it slapped the underside of my right bicep.

By the time I got around to the cockpit the arm was going numb. By the time I had taxied to the upper end of the airstrip the arm was turning yellow. With my "expert assistant" operating the manual flaps we had an uneventful trip home and I had a severely bruised arm to remind me of the escapade.

Such are the risks of hand propping. I would probably try to hand prop again in the same situation, but the risks are there and must be evaluated. The greatest danger of all may be an assistant who lies to you.

Years later I had another episode in the backcountry with a bad starter in a 182 with a 3-bladed prop. That time I elected not to attempt a hand prop, as I had never done it with a 3 blade. A friend came in who was more experienced, and with a qualified assistant, it fired right up. I never regretted that decision, as I was much older and had not hand propped in a long time.

Today, it seems batteries and even maintenance might be better than in the good old days, and I don't see much hand propping going on. But it's still an important skill to know, particularly if you like to explore the wilderness.

I was an Accident Prevention Counselor when this article was written. John Goostrey in the Boise FAA office was the Specialist and he was one of the rare good and helpful people in the agency. He sanctioned our first River of No Return Mountain Flying Seminar in 1987. The Wings program advanced from 5 to 7 phases and then died out for a number of years. It was revamped and is alive and well as of this writing. Here is a link to the URL for the FAA Wings Program today: www.faasafety.gov/WINGS/pub/learn_more. aspx

June 1986, Volume 4, Issue 6
Civilian Wings

Most civilian pilots use their wings and don't get to wear them, right? If you do happen to sport them on your chest, it's usually because they come with the costume—your snappy airlines uniform or your air force blouse. Maybe eventually oversize wings will come your way as a personal honor, along with a white robe, a halo, and golden slippers. But meanwhile, the only thing that could tell folks you fly, ordinarily, is your short shirt tail. There aren't that many elegant or tactful ways to reveal that you have a short shirt tail.

Well, fellow civilians, listen! The FAA would like us all not to rush and get measured for those heavenly pinions. The FAA invites us to wear their wings instead. I guarantee that earning the right to wear FAA wings is good insurance against a premature appointment with that saintly flight instructor Up Yonder.

The FAA has some smart, careful people figuring ways to keep us alive. One thing they've worked out in their new plan (it's been going since about 1979) is continuity. They evidently don't want a one-shot system that lets us earn our wings once and then gradually forget about safety as the months and years slip by. What they've developed is a graduated sequence over a (minimal) sixty-month period. We have to keep going back to them, and before they are through with us we're going to not only be permanently safety-minded, we're going to have some useful safety reflexes built into our hands, heads, eyes and feet.

They also don't make it too hard for us to get started: in just 120 days after the initial registration, a pilot can be wearing a handsome little FAA pin. Four more pins can follow, in due time. Those people are also cautious enough to make sure we don't get so carried away we wear all five sets at once. Each one outclasses its predecessor.

Phase I. Bronze wings

Phase II. Silver wings with a star

Phase III. Gold tone wings with star and wreath

Phase IV. Gold tone, simulated ruby

Phase V. Gold tone, rhinestone in the shield

They all come with certificates you can frame and hang in the office.

OK, so what do you do? Here's the scoop. Each phase of the five-step program can be completed every twelve months. To qualify, a pilot must attend an aviation related safety meeting conducted by an Accident Prevention Specialist or an Accident Prevention Counselor. (Any FAA office can tell you all the meeting dates and places). In addition, for each phase, three hours of dual instruction with a CFI are required within 120 days of beginning training under this program. After logging your three hours of CFI dual and attending an FAA-sanctioned safety seminar, you receive a set of wings and certificate for the appropriate phase.

As you see, the program has an economical two-for-one feature—one used by many pilots. You know that every pilot is required to have a biennial flight review (BFR) every twenty-four months. You can use the Wings Program to take care of the BFR because its CFI check rides are an acceptable substitute. Or vice-versa—the BFR could help you get started in the Wings Program. In my own participation, I have just completed Phase II of the Wings Program. I appreciate the feature that I can both stay current and make progress in Wings. And it is not only useful to get the evaluations of other professional pilots—it is necessary.

Airline pilots have to get refresher training regularly, and check rides every six months. Military pilots have similar training and recurrency checks. Air taxi and corporate pilots receive at least yearly training and checks. The private pilot, generally with less flight experience and money to fly regularly, is the one who needs and deserves the most training and receives the least. The Wings Program offers an incentive to even up the score and give general aviation the same high safety record that air carriers and other professionals have.

I've been fortunate enough to spend the equivalent of nearly eight hundred, eight-hour days at piloting, and love it. On the basis of that experience I can make a few points about your BFR, which is designed as a currency or training session, not as a test or check ride. You cannot "bust" a BFR. So no one needs to get uptight about one. You can make it a fun session as well as one you get something useful out of. Try telling your CFI what you feel rusty on, want to learn, or have never really understood before.

Look, Jack Nicklaus just won his sixth Master's Tournament, and he figured that a few tips from his caddy (a son) made the difference. If Jack Nicklaus can accept a few pointers gracefully, the rest of us lesser mortals needn't be too stiff-necked and negative.

My father's editorial and literature skills are quite evident in this article.

July/August 1986, Volume 4, Issue 7
Wait & Balance

Mark Twain told a sad story of over-loading; not a Cub but a frog named Dan'l, who could ordinarily outjump any other frog in Calveras County. A sizeable bet was on, and a sneaky stranger had managed to fill Dan'l with quail shot and set him on the floor at the starting line. Smiley, Dan'l's owner, started the contest.

"'One-two-three-jump!' and him and the feller touched up the frogs from behind, and the new frog hopped off, but Dan'l give a heave, and hysted up his shoulders-so-like a Frenchman, but it wa'n't no use—couldn't budge; he was planted as solid as an anvil, and he couldn't no more stir than if he was anchored out."

Some stranger might snicker and say, "Maybe you can weight down a frog, but you can't overload a Cub!" He might tell you plainly that whatever goes inside that doughty little airplane gets flown, no matter what. A nice affirmation of faith, but if you're going to bet on your Cub, you oughtn't to believe tales like that from a stranger. You'd better be very, very careful of who puts what in your Cub—and where.

Overload your Cub's nose, make it fly tail light, for instance, and you're asking for not just poor performance, but a high stall speed. Go the opposite way, tail heavy, and if you can keep the plane stable long enough to practice a stall, don't practice it anyway, because you might never recover. Do everything in balance, just overload your plane, and you're still in for the kind of bad flying, and possible grief, we demonstrated in an earlier issue.

Could you be talked into doing a few friendly little weight exercises? Even if you already sense your plane's center of gravity (C.G.) like a tightrope walker, fly like Jonathan Seagull, and estimate poundage like a butcher, you can still coax improved performance out of your plane. And better yet, you can know what to expect of it. There are enough uncertainties in flying without guessing about things you don't have to guess about.

Before we get into problems, let's think about basic overloading. To avoid that what we have to know, besides the weight of passengers and baggage, are the plane's empty weight (EW), the fuel and oil weights, and two maximum gross figures: "Normal" weight maximum, and "Utility" weight maximum. For the Cub, the normal maximum is 1750 pounds, and utility maximum (for mild aerobatics) is 1500.

If our plane's EW (empty weight) is 1075 pounds, fuel weighs six pounds a gallon, and seven quarts of oil weighs 12.5 pounds, what's left? Suppose you weigh 200 pounds and your passenger weights 250, plus 50 pounds of baggage.

The total is 1803.5. Oops! 53.5 pounds over maximum. If it's also hot weather and high altitude, why don't you triple your flight insurance?

Now, let's get to the balance problems. We are dealing with leverages, in a way the same kinds that operate a teeter-totter. If you fastened different weights to various places on a plank and wanted to pick that board up at its point of balance, you could do some arithmetic and figure out where that point of balance was. That's the kind of calculation we're working out here. There is a safe range for a Cub's center of gravity (the CG is always moving slightly, just by the consumption of fuel). So, a good pilot has to be certain of being within that safe range, the "envelope."

How do we stay within it? What we need to know next is a little more sophisticated. We have to calculate "leverages" (moments) which are the results of multiplying weights by distances from a standard, fixed, arbitrary vertical line. Those distances are called "arms" and the vertical line is the "datum." Here is where it gets doubly (or triply) tricky for Cub pilots. Piper, in its infinite wisdom, moved the datum some distance forward on all the "Cub series," and for the PA-18 Super Cub it happens to be 60" forward of the WLE (wing leading edge), which leads to the even more confusing number of 62.25" forward of the main wheels, where the actual weighing commonly takes place! For one of the simplest aircraft ever built, this makes the weight & balance one of the most difficult. (I spend less time doing weight & balance problems on transport category aircraft!)

LOCK HAVEN, PENNA.   PAGE 4
                     PA-18"150"
                     MODEL PA-18A"150'

PIPER AIRCRAFT CORPORATION

LOCK HAVEN, PENNSYLVANIA

ACTUAL WEIGHT AND BALANCE

MODEL PA-18"150", MODEL PA-18A"150"

SERIAL NO. 18-   CERTIFICATE NO. N   DATE

AIRPLANE WEIGHING DIAGRAM

Empty Weight as Weighed (Includes items checked on Pages 7, 8, & 9.)

	Scale Reading	Tare	Net
Left Wheel	_____	_____	_____
Right Wheel	_____	_____	_____
Tail Scale (N)	_____	_____	_____
Total (T)			_____

Revised: June 21, 1960.
         November 15, 1960
         August 23, 1963
580 820 August 28, 1963
         August 12, 1974

PREPARED _____
CHECKED _____
APPROVED _____

Now let's pick up some information we were using earlier, add arm measurements, and do some multiplying.

ITEM	WEIGHT	ARM	MOMENT
A/c EW	1,075	74.4	79,980
Oil	15	24	360
Fuel (18 gal)	110	84	9,240
Front Seat	180	97	12,780
Rear Seat	180	117	17,460
Baggage (STC'd)	170	117	19,890
Ext. Baggage (STC'd)	20	146	2,920
Total	1,750	659.4	142,630

Now it's time to divide. If we divide the moment by the total weight, we get the distance the loaded CG is from the datum: 142630 divided by 1750 is 81.5 inches. The "envelope" shows what the safe and acceptable distances are between the loaded CG and the EWCG. For a PA-18 the datum is 60" ahead of the wing leading edge, and the main wheel center line is 2.25" behind the wing leading edge. This is the "arbitrary vertical line" used for calculations, so we subtract 62.25 from 81.5, and get 19.2". Look up that figure in the envelope, and you see that the gross weight puts us on the upper line of the normal range and 19.2 puts us close to the far-right line.

If we lose a quart of oil (5 lbs), add 12 gallons of fuel (70 lbs), the pilot adds 5 lb. of clothing, the rear seat adds 70 lb of baggage, and another 15 lb. of stuff is left out of the extended baggage, we would end up with the same weight but a CG of 16.8", a much better performance pattern.

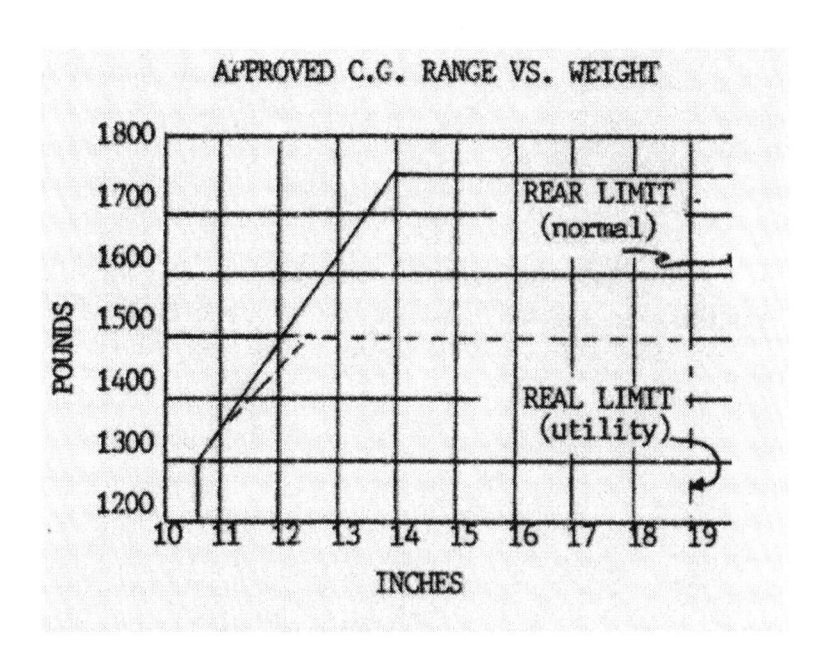

APPROVED C.G. RANGE VS. WEIGHT

September 1986, Volume 4, Issue 8
Part II Wait & Balance

Last month, we started on some weight and balance problems and examples. Let's continue and see what we have to do to operate in the utility category, where our max weight will be 1500 and our max aft CG is 19 instead of 20. In the normal category, you are guaranteed that the wings and fuselage can withstand 3.8 times the gross weight of 1750 in positive G's, or a 6650-pound load. In the utility category, for mild acrobatics, you are guaranteed 4.4 times the gross weight of 1500 (positive G's only), or a 6600-pound load. In the restricted category, as a sprayer, the gross weight is actually 2000 lbs. But we all knew ag flying was dangerous and the pilots were crazy anyway, right? The point is that being overweight, while perhaps not as crucial as being out of balance, can structurally damage your bird, particularly in turbulence. And it will definitely affect the performance, even to the point of getting no performance.

So, downloading the fuel a little and emptying the baggage compartment (who wants stuff floating around back there, anyway?) enables us to go practice spins, chandelles, lazy eights, or steep turns over 60 degrees bank. If you decide to do loops or hammerheads with negative G's, you're on your own because you've just become a test pilot. I don't know about you, but they don't pay me enough for that stuff, and I don't own a parachute.

Doing some calculations might surprise you. You won't make 1500 lbs. without tiny pilots and minimum fuel. The Cub is simply not meant to be an aerobatic airplane.

Remember these basics for a weight and balance problem:
1. Weight X Arm = Moment
2. Total moments divided by total weight = loaded CG distance from datum
3. The result of #2 minus 62.3"= inches aft of datum
4. GW determines abscissa (horizontal) line in envelope

This kind of counting takes just a little extra time. But it makes flying your Cub a better bet.

I could lecture for hours about over gross operations, but the following story says it all, in language all bush operators will understand:

Norwegian Hunting Story

This was gleaned from the EAA newsletter *The Taildragger*. Jerry Davis of Corvallis reported that it was taken from a Minnesota newspaper.

Big Ole stopped by the other day, and we were talking about hunting.

"Ven yew go moose hunting in de fall, do yew fly vit vone uf dem bush pilots to a camp in de voods?" Ole asked.

"That's right," I told my Norwegian friend.

"Me and Lars used to fly in, too."

"You did? Ever have any luck?" I questioned.

"Yew bet. Shot many moose, but ve finally gif it up."

"How come?"

"Vell, last time ve vas up dere, bush pilot drops us off und den leaves. Lars und Ay, ve go out hunting couple hours und ve bag two big bull moose. Ho boy, ve sure vas lucky. Ve spent next couple days vaiting for aeroplane and celebrating vit little nip now und den from snake bite kit. Finally aeroplane pilot come back for us. "No, too big a load," he says."

"Nay, nay, nay," says Lars, "we've done it last year. Ve tie vone moose onde vone ving und de odder moose on de odder ving. Dat distributes de veight."

"Vell, Ay am here to tell yew, dat pilot, he vas less den happy vit de situation, but he finally straps moose onto de vings, me und Lars und all our gear get into aeroplane, und ve take off down de lake. Ve must haf run down de vater couple miles before pilot gets her up in de air. Ve get up to about 700 feet ven all uf a sudden aeroplane nosedive straight back into lake."

"Uff da, it was terrible!" Ole continued. "Ve lost evert'ing. Pilot, aeroplane, our gear, moose, whole vorks sinks. Me und Lars vaslucky, though, ve got out uf aeroplane und svim to shore. As we vas laying dere catching our breath, Lars gets confused look on his face. "V-v-vere are ve?" je asks."

"Near as Ay can figger, ve made it 'bout hunert feet furder den ve did last year,' Ay tell him.

October/November 1986, Volume 4, Issue 9
Survival

  In late November, 1979, a friend was flying the last of a hunting camp out of Cold Meadows, a 7000-foot-high airstrip in the Idaho Wilderness. The deserted camp was covered with about 10 inches of snow. My friend, a 9000-hour bush pilot, had been one of the original Alaska Fish and Game Super Cub pilot/conservation officers. Well aware of the risks, he had dressed in wool from head to toe, and was wearing good boots. When I talked to him after his second run, he wasn't happy with snow conditions, but felt pressured to return in late afternoon for the last load. He had no extra survival gear with him.

  After dark, when I was home showering, his wife called. He wasn't back. I rounded up a Cessna 206 (wishing I had a Cub available), a friend, and a survival pack. We filled three thicknesses of garbage bags with materials: newspaper, matches, instant soup, coffee, candy bars, blankets, and first aid gear. We used duct tape to tie up the bundle.

  We headed off to Cold Meadows. The crystal-clear sky, with no moon, was dark as the inside of a cow, as they say. Other less publishable comparisons could describe the temperature. That night the town of Stanley, 1000 feet lower, reported -25°F.

  At Cold Meadows, in the dark, we made a low pass down the airstrip, with lighting at a minimum to retain night vision. One of us flew visually with the other calling out airspeed and altitude. We were down below the treetops, doing perhaps the trickiest flying we had ever attempted.

The minimum lighting idea didn't work. It was impossible to distinguish anything on the ground. When we finally hit the landing lights, there was the 206 upside down in the snow. We pulled up for another pass to drop the survival gear. My flying buddy suggested taping our lighted flashlight to the pack, which we did. Down below the trees again, we made what felt like a good drop, but still saw no sign of life. (Actually, the pilot had lit a small fire at the campsite in the timber, and he said later that the shock of a 206 suddenly appearing from behind the ridge, lights blazing, had taken him completely by surprise).

We pulled up again, and after discussing the risks decided to make one more pass. This time we saw the pilot (Carl Branham) in front of the airplane, waving his arms. Ecstatic, we headed home.

Carl had not observed the airdrop, but he saw the flashlight twinkling out of the snow and found the pack about ten yards from his aircraft. He told me, eventually, that the equipment had probably saved his life. But his response the next day was laconic, as he was being flown out by Bill Dorris of McCall in a ski plane. I was doing some other charter work and were in touch by radio. "You okay, Carl?" The familiar gravelly understatement came back, "Well, I'll tell you, Dick, Cold Meadows is the right name for that place." While I was thinking over that summary, he added, "You could of stuck cigarettes and whiskey in that pack."

Maybe I would have added cigarettes, if there had been time. But not whiskey. You are not likely to get any two pilots to agree exactly on what should be in a survival pack. But I have now had seven years to think about the episode, and some things that made a crucial difference.

What you select must vary according to place, season, and personal needs, and your options fall under four general headings:

1. Apparel and personally carried items
2. First aid supplies
3. Provisions
4. Additional survival equipment

In next month's column, continuing this topic, I have expanded the four headings somewhat, with the object of getting at the choices a pilot must make. You should be able to apply the experience of others to your own circumstances, so you don't blindly follow anyone's example. In next month's column we will also look again at Carl's survival. What items in the four lists helped to keep him alive? How? Then we will try to apply those lessons to your choice of items to wear and carry in your Cub.

This story is told in full in "Notes From The Cockpit" (R.K. Williams, 2015).

December 1986, Volume 4, Issue 10
Survival Part II

Last month I recorded the survival of a pilot after a crash in -30ºF weather at Cold Meadows airstrip. A number of things combined to save his life: they mostly fall under the four headings of clothing and personally carried items, first aid supplies, provisions, and additional survival equipment. No single combination of items will cover all the possible problems, so you have to think about your potential enemies in advance and prepare for the most likely ones. In a survival situation your opponents could be isolation, starvation, a life-threatening injury with severe bleeding, cold, shock, physical weakness, disorientation, thirst—and you, yourself. (If you lose your cool and determination you will almost certainly become a hazard to yourself. So make your lists with that factor in mind: what will help to keep ME confident and resolute?)

1. Clothing and apparel. Carl knew that proper clothing is the first line of defense against a whole range of dangers—severe weather, immediate loss of energy, sun, moisture. He also knew that wool provides classic insulation. Several layers of light material were much better than a single ply of heavy stuff. The buck knife Carl wore on his belt proved to be his best tool. He had matches in his pocket, and those could have been what kept him alive until our help came. The jacket he had tossed in his 206 also made a crucial difference after the sun went down.

2. It so happened that Carl was lucky enough not to need a first aid kit, but let's think about this item, anyway. A standard Coghlan's Pack III kit comes in a plastic bag and fits in the seat pocket. Admittedly, it's not much, but it doesn't take up much room or weight, either. The size of your kit may vary according to your knowledge. If you are in real medical trouble, band aids and aspirin won't help you. But neither will sophisticated equipment you don't understand. Better take some first-aid training that makes you resourceful in emergencies—able to use a belt properly as a tourniquet, for example. Add to your kit what you know could help you cope with a bad injury. Don't scorn aspirin and band aids, either, or insect repellent in some seasons and places; they could make a contribution to your morale.

Some heroes of World War II (according to my father), recounting their invasion of a Pacific island, remembered that gnats bothered them more than the shells they were facing. "It's the LITTLE things that get you down," they agreed. A few band aids and a vial of cutters, in an emergency, could help reverse a despairing mood.

Carl jokingly scolded me for not providing the "first aid" of whiskey and cigarettes. His responses showed that he hadn't lost his perspective or sense of humor. Those are among the most valuable assets you can have when you're in trouble.

3. The provisions we dropped to Carl in our survival pack included instant soup, coffee, and candy bars for restoration of body heat and quick energy. These were

obviously designed to help someone who had already been found. IF Carl had had a survival pack in his plane, and IF we hadn't found him for several days he would have had emergency food, for sure, like cereal and jerky, but he would also have had the means of getting more food—a gun and fish line and hooks. That's backpacker wisdom, and it's good.

4. As to extra gear, in harsh months I carry snowshoes, wing covers, and an old Boy Scout pack with the following:
.38 pistol with bird shot and regular lead
Hunting and army knife
Jerky
Ace bandages
Extra eyeglasses
Sleeping bag
Wool cap, socks and pants
Long johns
Garbage sack
Toilet Paper
Flares
String
2 space blankets
Water tablets
Matches, newspaper
Ski gloves
Another Coghlan's Pack III first aid kit
Book: *Survival Sense For Pilots* by Robert Stoffel and Patrick LaVolla

Because the pack is fairly heavy and bulky, I've been tempted to leave it out occasionally. But I don't unless the cargo includes similar materials. Some of the above items probably, also, saved Carl's life.

Two other permanent aids are a canteen and bag of tools strapped underneath the back seat. There are, of course, many commercial survival kits on the market. They are quite expensive and fairly large. Cub Crafters sells an interesting one, called Survival Unlimited, a three-way pack that zips together. One pack is food, another is first aid, and the third is other equipment. Unique Project's Survival-6-Pak appears to be another good commercial survival kit.

The Super Cub, limited by its size, has some special considerations regarding survival gear. Because of this, put some thought into what you are wearing and carrying on your person. I always carry a coffee can with the following equipment:

Survival kit list for 2.5 pound coffee can
#18 wire
20' of twine
2 small trash bags, 1 large
2 small ziplock bags, 1 large
1 fiber towel
5 tissues
1 moist towelette
1 soap
1 alcohol sponge
5 bandaids
Single edge razor blade
Mirror

Whistle
Notepad and crayon
3 safety pins
Matches
10 aspirin
8 sugar packs
3 salt tablets
3 creamers
Vitamins
Small can
2 candles
Bouillon cubes
Soup mix or Ramen
Candy
Cereal and meat bars
Chocolate bars
Compass
Water tablets
50' fishing line
Hooks, weights, leaders
Insect repellant
Lip balm
Vaseline
Ammonia inhalants
Coins for phone
Hacksaw blade
Pocket knife
Space blanket
Coffee packs
3' of 3" clear plastic surgical tubing
Fire starter
3 pieces aluminum foil

Fill the can with beans and rice, and tape. You can get most of this in, but you may have to set some priorities. Remember to set priorities according to the circumstances. And, of course, the less you have to use the stuff, the better.

Well, it is pretty obvious that this was written a while ago. You probably don't need coins for a pay phone these days! But a lot of the information and theory is still valid, and I still have that old coffee can in the back of the Cub! Remember that survival gear should be personalized, based on the geographic area, and seasonal.

January 1987, Volume 5, Issue 1
Rehearsals and Realities

At a fly-in contest last spring, ten commercial pilots were required to make two power-off spot landings, one with full flaps and one with no flaps. The challenge proved to be an eye opener. Every pilot, including me, landed short and was disqualified (at least I qualified on **one** of the two landings). Naturally, ten commercial pilots could produce twenty plausible excuses, and a couple of good reasons. In backcountry and in short field landings, we habitually use power-on landings for a controlled approach. And in the interest of engine care we rarely make a power-off approach to pavement, because during steep descents into valleys and canyons, we want to prevent thermal shock.

In a real emergency we would know enough to give ourselves a fudge factor; and in "practice emergencies" we do the same thing by aiming about a third of the way down from the approach end. Then we tend to overlook or forgive a mediocre performance. But the contest demonstrated how rusty our emergency techniques had become. I left the contest vowing to practice power-off spot landings myself, and to regularly have students, BFR candidates, and recurrent pilots practice them also. (Inevitably, the first two or three tries, they all land short).

I recommend that you rehearse some power-off spot landings. Someday, if you happen to be heading for a safe landing spot with a dead motor, you'll be a lot more likely to reach it if you've practiced in an unforgiving frame of mind. And you will probably go a lot farther as a pilot if you develop and practice a "daily rehearsal" philosophy.

I teach "daily rehearsal" emergency procedures early in a pilot's training, and still practice them myself every day I fly. For single engine carbureted aircraft, the five memorized, habitualized, automatic actions are carb heat, best glide speed, place to land, re-start, and shut down. The first three can be done simultaneously, and often there won't be time for anything else. I go through these five items in my mind, but I don't actually pull the power and lose altitude. I assure myself that I will automatically cover those five items, and I spend a lot of time evaluating and critiquing my landing choice as I fly on by. Was a better one available, or was I going to land downhill or downwind? What could I have seen as I got closer, and what could I have changed throughout the approach? I believe in this daily routine; I have proved that it works in two actual power plant failures.

For items four and five, re-start includes changing tanks, checking mags and adjusting mixture (turning mags off and on or leaning mixture can induce a backfire which may blow ice out of the carb). Shutdown includes fuel off, mixture lean, mags off, master off after emergency radio call, and seatbelt tightened.

An acquaintance of mine was killed recently in the backcountry after a power plant failure during takeoff. His fatal error, which a little safety rehearsal might have taught him to avoid, was attempting to turn back to the strip instead of opting for terrain straight ahead. That number one no-no, trying a dead motor 180 turn without sufficient altitude, has killed literally hundreds of pilots.

What is sufficient altitude? The answer varies with aircraft, wind, terrain, and load. In a sailplane, 200 feet

AGL will be the absolute minimum. In an empty 206, 600 to 700 feet are minimal. In a Super Cub, my rule is 500 feet, assuming the nose is up at Vy, with full power at the moment of power loss, and no wind. (When conditions allow, I move over to the right as soon as practical after takeoff, to be able to do a true 180 back to the runway instead of a 270 or more. That initial safety adjustment is not always feasible when other traffic is on downwind).

For the sake of your future safety, don't neglect such procedures in conjunction with power-off landings. Watch your altimeter and see how much altitude and room you really need to complete a 180 or a 270 compound turn after the power is at idle.

Part 91.199 of the FAR states that a passenger briefing is required for all occupants not familiar with the aircraft. This includes smoking, use of seat belts, emergency exits, survival gear, ditching over water, and use of oxygen. I suggest you heed this FAR, especially well; pilots have been sued for failing to give adequate briefings. One suit in particular grew out of a floatplane accident in which a passenger drowned because he did not know how to open the aircraft door. Passengers need safety rehearsals too.

The best pilots I know have the habit of practicing and learning. Take Tom Hutchison and Chris Christensen, for instance. Tom is probably one of the highest time Super Cub pilots in the world today. He has spent 11,000 hours in Cubs, with 10,000 hours of time coyote hunting. He is the head of all government aerial hunting in the Western United States. Chris has a combined total of 15,000 hours crop-dusting and hunting.

Both of these men have coyote hunting down to

an art. Watching and flying with these professionals really makes one realize how specialized low slow hunting flying is. But I have always been convinced that even high time pilots need specialized dual instruction before successfully and safely attempting this type of flying. What is interesting about both Tom and Chris is that they learn something from every flight they make, and they never seem to quit practicing. I think they keep their eyes and ears open to learn from other pilots. I think they pay attention to what they're doing every second, they are unexcitable, analytical, wary, and respectful, and also probably lucky. Although luck is tough to define and impossible to depend on, I will explore it more in the future. It might even be possible to practice being lucky.

I hunted coyotes for a number of years as a contract pilot for a government agency. I watched as high-time pilots for the agency had fatal accidents and was appointed to lead a national blue-ribbon panel to study the problem and come up with possible solutions. It was a well put together panel with fixed wing and rotary wing experts from U.S. Fish & Wildlife, Border Patrol, and Washington, D.C., and after presenting our findings six months later we were awarded for a "Substantial Contribution to Aviation Safety" from the Secretary of Agriculture. It was a worthwhile study and resulted in a safer, better funded organization.

One of our concerns was that pilots could be running into their own wake turbulence, and we explored than more in depth in the book "Mountain, Canyon, and Backcountry Flying" (Hoover and Williams, 2019).

This old article once again shows how much things have changed over the years. When I bought my Cub in 1981 I counted about six other Cubs in the entire state of Idaho. Today there still aren't a lot of certified Cubs around, but there are dozens of experimental Cubs as well as small, STOL, Cub-like aircraft around. And off-field landings have become extremely popular everywhere.

February 1987, Volume 5, Issue 2
Off-Field Operations

Ever since people could talk, it seems they talked about flying, but in spite of brilliant artist-planners like Leonardo Di Vinci, they never successfully did anything about powered flight until about eighty years ago. Only eighty years—and the Cub first appeared forty years ago!

Today, after four decades that have included moonshots, shuttles, and the Rutans' "Voyager", the Cub remains famous for doing exactly what it was designed to do, and better than any recent substitute. The old workhorse DC-3 is giving place to Twin Otters. High performance F-16s have long since replaced the once-deadly P-51s. But for grasshopper duty, off-field operations, you still can't beat the Cub, one of the few good old airplanes still holding their own. The Cub can't go straight up, it can't hover, it can't move at 400 MPH in level flight, it can't carry four passengers. But it can get you into exclusive places, as not only a great and economical flier, but a great and economical lander.

Off-field operations, once commonplace during

the barnstorming days, are virtually a lost art that can be performed safely nowadays by only a select aircraft, principally the Cub. In the last forty years, though, a lot of power and telephone lines, fences, and ditches have appeared-besides additional crops that farmers tend to be quite protective of. So the problems of off-field operations have increased to the point that most insurance policies do not cover them.

In off-field flying, landings present most of the unusual hazards, and the pilot's job is to give the plane a chance to do its thing-without interruptions. The pilot must spot and avoid unusual dangers as systematically as possible. Some techniques can greatly assist you.

1. *The three-tier approach to a landing site.*

In the first and highest tier (50-800'AGL) the pilot evaluates approach and departure paths, particularly departure, because it's hard to see once you're on the ground. It is also necessary to assess wind, length of run, and hazards such as trees and power lines.

The second tier is from 5-50' AGL. At that level the pilot can spot snow markers, highway signs, fences, and high terrain alongside the landing track that could strike the wingtips.

The third tier is the landing surface itself. A low pass allows inspection for width, rocks, holes, ditches, logs, ruts, and slope. Use your passenger's help during the entire procedure, and if you're not sure about the landing site, go somewhere else.

2. Surface evaluations

Off field landing surfaces are extremely varied. Experience and extreme caution are necessary in learning to evaluate them. The best way is to get to the area by ground travel and walk the track. Though that's not often feasible, a good pilot will never scorn the safest solution. Each type of surface has its own problems.

a. Paved highways are littered with traffic, power lines, highway signs, and snow markers. Therefore, they are generally not a good choice, except for night emergencies.

b. Dirt roads have ruts, power lines, occasional signposts, some traffic, and sometimes high fences or terrain off-side.

c. Jeep trails have treacherous ruts, rough terrain, often poor wingtip clearance, and narrow main gear tracks.

d. Pastures and fields have crops, irrigation ditches or pipes, plowing furrows and fences.

e. Desert patches are notorious for rocks, holes and sagebrush that can be surprisingly tall and tough.

f. Mountain ridges also specialize in the above, with the addition of squirrelly winds and steep slopes.

g. Gravel bars require concern about length and rock size.

h. Beaches present the added factors of wind, slope and sand firmness.

i. Frozen lakes. Besides the obvious dangers of ice that is too thin, too soft, or spotty, frozen lakes offer the hazard of wind-blown ridges.

3. Training

Don't attempt off-field landings unless you are very comfortable at crosswind, stall and wheel landings. Directional control can be very marginal on narrow, rutted, or muddy surfaces. If you think you may ever have to land off-field, practice all types of landings on a regular airstrip and try to get some appropriate dual out in the boondocks.

Why do off-field landings? Well, who know when you will discover the perfect fishing hole? Or picnic spot? Or when the holding tank won't outlast the gas tank? Or when you won't have a choice about landing quickly?

For another thing, off-field landings are fun. You get the satisfaction in using your airplane for what it is good at, low flying, and landing. You can shut it down and enjoy the desert or prairie silence with no other airplanes around. Another Cub companion might be fine, I guess, but a lot of Cubbers tend to be loners when it comes to other, fancy airplanes—those youngsters that haven't been around for forty years.

Luck, particularly in aviation, is a concept I have been fascinated with for years. Ernest Gann, in "Fate Is the Hunter," delved into the subject as well as anyone. But, with help from my father, I think we did okay in this little treatise, and it is one of my favorites.

March 1987, Volume 5, Issue 3
Riding with Lady Luck

One of the most outrageous statements I have ever heard of came from a commercial pilot whose passengers had just barely escaped death or serious injury. He had attempted an incredibly stupid takeoff: over gross, from a short canyon airstrip, with a temperature of 95°F. After barely making it across the river he had been "lucky" enough to reach a flat bench to crash on. The plane had somersaulted, turned upside down. The passengers crawled out with minor injuries. The pilot told them, "Well, you're just lucky that you had a pilot as good as me behind the controls."

Let's sort it out. What he should have said was, "Ladies and gentlemen, you have just experienced the memorable performance of a pilot with world class good luck. I'm a flying cat who's been blessed with nine lives, and I've just used up my fifth. A survival rate like mine makes up for many deficits in skill, judgement and knowledge!"

On the other hand, he should also have levelled with the passengers: "Of course, ladies and gentlemen, I concede that you have been unlucky. With a little better help from the stars you might have flown this run with a competent pilot." He would at least have been correct in pointing out that there's good luck and there's bad luck. A person really ought to be clear about that much, and about which is which.

There are so many uncertainties in this world, an element of luck appears to be not just part of aviation, but part of every activity and occupation; scorned, perhaps, and relied on more in some fields than others, but still there in them all.

If it weren't for bad luck, I'd have no luck at all.

Some pilots are unlucky. They are the ones who happen to fly the airplane when the wheel bolts break after five other pilots just got through flying it. They are the ones who get the flight that the crankshaft breaks on. They arrive at the airport ten minutes after the fog does. They may be only partially unlucky, or partially lucky, because they don't get injured seriously or they have another place to land. Perhaps there are not many truly unlucky pilots around to talk about it. Some, I think, realize they are unlucky, at least partially and either fly accordingly or quit altogether. Analyzing your luck, along with your skill and knowledge, has to do with setting your own personal limitations.

When the Emperor Napoleon Bonaparte would organize his troops and pick new generals, the last question he would ask a candidate was, "Are you lucky?" What was he actually getting at, I wonder. Was he trying to spot and avoid the unlucky loser, the officer whose horse will drop a shoe nail at an inconvenient time, like when a battle is at stake? Was he looking for cool gentlemen who didn't believe in luck? Was he seriously hoping to select lucky soldiers? Was he secretly aiming to weed out people like the "nine lives pilot," who survived on luck, not ability? Maybe, even, he wanted to eliminate the men who passed off their own inadequacy as "bad luck". We'll never know.

But maybe he had something in common with Chuck Yeager, who attributed his longevity and success as a pilot not to "the right stuff," but to luck and experience. And somehow, he must have had the right attitude toward that temptress, the goddess Lady Luck. It is said that if you spurn her, she will return to you, cringing and fawning; if you court her, she will turn on you savagely.

Chuck Yeager must have had exactly the right touch, scorning Lady Luck and spitting in her face. Maybe he also had something in common with mail carriers who know their business, and that includes knowing where to expect trouble, and understanding the art of coping with treacherous animals.

A Few Crosswinds

The June article on emergencies touched off some interesting questions and responses. It's a pleasure to concentrate this issue on an Alaskan reader who took the trouble to bring up three especially salient points: Tom Prunty of Chugiak, Alaska.

Tom asks, "When you're talking sequences to follow in the event of engine failure, why not mention switching tanks?" He argues, "Many temporary engine failures result from running a tank dry. If a Cub driver reaches for the selector valve first he may solve a problem before it becomes serious…" As you know, Tom, I mentioned the need to think of the dry tank possibility, in the first sentence following the checklist. I didn't make it part of the checklist itself because a shift in tanks might not be an automatic procedure. But you're absolutely right in emphasizing the point; never overlook the dry tank possibility. Maybe you and I can work out together a six-step sequence to include a gas check.

Tom also questions my suggestion that at level or descending power off flight, "a momentary climb to best glide speed could buy you an important couple of hundred feet." Tom reasoned, "The momentary climb will cause additional drag and actually shorten your over-all glide distance." He adds that to ask someone in an emergency situation to pull back on the stick appears to be a bad judgment call," and would rather ask the pilot to reach optimum glide speed by pushing the nose over or else by holding level flight until best glide speed is reached.

Again, the perspective of an obvious professional is appreciated. It tells me it would have been well to preface my "momentary climb" recommendation with an explanation that this point is sometimes argued among flying instructors as they try to settle how much to tell an inexperienced pilot. They don't want to lead a student into an inadvertent stall, and yet they don't want to deprive that pilot of what might be a life-saving extra bit of distance. Tom Prunty's response can help a reader to understand that my recommendation is a device for pushing an aircraft to its performance limits in an emergency, but also a device that could trap a beginner or clumsy pilot into a stall. As for Tom's claim that a momentary climb will actually shorten the glide distance because of additional drag, this is another point that has been long debated in flying circles, with no clear-cut answer either way. I know that the opposite, also debated, holds true. In trying to lengthen a glide or tweak over an obstacle, a momentary descent for a little extra speed, or application of partial to full flap (manual control), just before the critical point, will help to hop the fence, hedge, or what have you. I have never had to use that technique in an actual emergency, but I have friends who have, and they swear by it. I definitely keep it in my bag of tricks.

Finally, Tom has questioned the principle that best glide speed increases with a headwind and decreases with a tailwind. He joins the company of a number of experienced professionals who have doubted the principle, which could be the basis of a good trick question or two. But a serious consideration is at issue, and Tom's challenge on this point clearly demonstrates that more discussion is in order.

One court of appeal is Mike Stockhill, former FAA and NTSB official and longtime general aviation pilot. You may have seen some of his feature articles in *Private Pilot* magazine. Mike reduces the issue to the practical question of why you need to increase glide speed in a headwind: "If your best glide speed is 50, and you have a 50-mph headwind, how far are you going to glide?" If you exceed your best glide speed you will sacrifice some hypothetical distance, but at least you will travel some real distance. Mike's 727 experience included the use of graphs to calculate best glide descents in relation to both fuel burn and wind direction.

Another court of appeal is *"The Joy of Soaring,"* by Carle Conway, a book long respected as the glider pilot's bible. In a section titled, "Best Glide speed and Speed-To-Fly," Conway writes, "…Best Glide speed is a term that was long ago preempted by the aviation industry to signify the indicated airspeed which results in the flattest glide angle for a particular glider in still air…in a final glide, then head and tailwinds do affect the speed for flattest glide. Headwinds require a faster glide, and tailwinds a slower one."

The correct term for this speed is simply speed-to-fly in wind. The exact value is a matter of arithmetic (or graphic solution) provided one knows accurately what the wind is. As a practical matter, the glider pilot usually has only a rough notion of the wind at his altitude, so precise calculations are rather futile. A reasonably good approximation is sufficient. Here is a rule of thumb: for headwinds, speed up by half the estimated headwind, keeping the estimate on the high side; for tailwind, slow down by half the estimated tailwind, keeping the estimate on the low side, but never fly slower than the speed for minimum sink.*

*The reader may notice the inconsistency with the advice given the newly soloed student. The benefit of flying slower in a tailwind is trifling, and it was not thought wise to ask a pilot at this level of experience to remember so much.

Conway also wished to cut through theoretical definitions to get down to practical advice on how to handle a glider under varying wind conditions. At an altitude of 8000' a Cub operating without power is obviously going to have to be treated like a glider. Just as Conway in an appendix has different speeds graphed out for one particular glider, some aircraft manuals offer best glide tables based on gross weight, sea level, zero wind. A pilot needs to understand how to add to and apply those figures in the unlikely event that his power aircraft suddenly has become a glider.

We have seen one study, done by a Super Cubber on floats, that indicates glide speed does not change in the wind until the wind velocities are forty knots or better. However, the computerized study isn't controlled in that it doesn't test the published best glide speed, the gross weight is unknown, the altitude is unknown, it's on floats, were the gauges accurate, etc. However, it is still a very interesting study that makes us wonder if more work shouldn't be done in this area. Personally, if the need arises, I intend to slightly raise airspeed in a headwind and decrease it in a tailwind.

One final safety thought, relating to changing seasons. As fall weather brings hunting season near, remember that, statistically, this is a dangerous time. Please take a look at Gerry Bruder's thoughtful article "Pressure Points," in AOPA, March 1987. This essay should get under every pilot's skin, private or professional. We are all susceptible to five recognizable attitudes that render flight relatively unsafe, the mindsets of anti-authority, machoism, impulsivity, invulnerability, and resignation. All of us have tendencies toward one or more of these traits. I'm anti-authority myself. Which are you? Recognition is the first step toward prevention.

Reader, please feel free to follow Tom Prunty's good example, and send along your reactions and experiences. The value of this column is multiplied by the participation of tried and true Cubbers.

It was inevitable to eventually run afoul of some readers, especially when touching on "touchy" subjects. Responding was often like walking on eggshells, keeping an open mind, not discouraging other ideas, but sometimes sticking to my (and every other professional's) guns when there was only one right answer. My father's expertise in tact and diplomacy was evident in this one.

Here are a couple of good links to a deeper explanation of glide speeds in wind:
http://studysoaring.stlsoar.org/aerodyn.htm
www.5c1.net/Glider%20Performance%20Airspeeds.htm

April 1987, Volume 5, Issue 4
Peaceful Uses of Flaps

One beautiful summer day a few years ago, in late afternoon, I was scooting over the mountains toward Mackay Bar, a Salmon River Canyon strip, to pick up a load of boaters. It was one of those relaxing flights, with me singing to the airplane, enjoying life, and it singing back. In crossing over the Chamberlain Basin airstrip (site of the 1984 Super Cub Pilot's Association fly-in), I noticed a low wing Piper taxiing down to the East. When it became evident that the pilot was about to take off to the West, my eyebrows went up an inch. The plane would have a slight headwind but be heading uphill toward rising terrain and into sinking air. Obviously, the pilot had not received any kind of checkout at this backcountry airstrip; an instructor would have explained those dangers even in an oral check. The aircraft was a worrisome choice, too: in high density altitude work, that short stubby low Piper wing just doesn't seem to develop a lift comparable to that of other shapes.

Though the Piper appeared to get airborne at the intersection of the two strips, I couldn't tell how badly it was climbing until it plunged right into the trees at the end of the strip. It was hard to believe what I had witnessed. Beginning a descent, I tuned in to 121.5 and, sure enough, there was the ELT. Being too low to reach FSS, I went ahead and landed, hoping not to be the first to reach the crash site. I thankfully saw that some campers at the end of the strip already had pulled people out of the airplane—a couple and two small boys. The worst problems appeared to be the woman's broken arm and her state of shock. The pilot, an FAA medical examiner, said something like this: "I took off with two notches of flaps. It wouldn't climb so I raised the flaps. Then it just settled back down and went right into the trees."

To an experienced bush pilot, the takeoff failure was fully explained. I loaded the family into the 185 and delivered them to McCall.

Accidents are usually the culmination of a chain of event or errors. First, the pilot had failed to get a proper checkout for the mountain field. Second, he had attempted to take off in the wrong direction. Third, the aircraft model was not ideal. Last, and most critical was improper use of flaps. Because flaps produce both lift and drag, their use in critical situations is complex. Most of what you get in aircraft manuals takeoff settings for normal and short field operations. In the real bush and backcountry world, those handbook recommendations often don't go far enough. Some of the statements are even controversial. For example, many STOL aircraft operate well in the takeoff mode with greater-than-recommended flap settings. For example, in Canada, the Canadian built Twin Otter uses 20 degrees flaps for a STOL takeoff. The ever-conservative U.S. FAA does not recognize STOL operations in the Otter, whose reputation in the backcountry is legendary. They demand 10-degree takeoffs for all 135 and 121 (commercial) operations. The figures in a flight manual are there for a reason, of course, and you invite trouble with insurance carriers and/or the FAA if you haven't operated within the stated limits. But those stats are not always the last word in critical aircraft operations.

Normal Operations
or
"By the Book Short Field Operations"

The Super Cub Owners Handbook has more practical wisdom about flap operation than most modern operator's manuals. On page 8, for example, "The flap lever can be set in any one of three positions, for full up flap, half flap, or full down flap. Full flap is recommended for minimum speed landings. Half or full flap can be applied to reduce takeoff run, the more flap used the shorter the run. A minimum takeoff distance is obtained by beginning the takeoff with flaps up, then applying full flaps when takeoff speed (30-35 mph) has been reached. The best angle of climb is attained with full flap. The best rate of climb is without any flap extended."

The procedure described here has to be considered standard short field operation, although I have some problems with it. For now, I'll say that this is the only aircraft handbook I have ever seen that talks about full flap takeoffs and climb outs for land planes. Most operator's manuals recommend a partial flap setting that produces maximum lift; that setting is used for takeoff and climb out over a 50' obstacle (Vx).

The chances are that's how you learned short field procedures. There's really nothing wrong with that setting for average short field work. If the doctor had followed that manual he would have had a chance, at least, to clear the first trees. (His aircraft might not have overcome the rising terrain and bad air, however, and actually, hitting trees at the end of the strip at slow speed was better than going down a mile away from help and at 150' AGL.)

But his immediate error was obvious; dumping flaps while in ground effect to try to gain lift. That action creates an impossible situation. The sudden loss of lift, without enough speed to leave ground effect, wipes out the possibility of remaining airborne.

So much for the good doctor. Let's talk about some special procedures (and at the end of this column are some special definitions if you need them).

Abnormal, or Special Procedures

First, not all Cubs have 3 notches of flaps (20, 37, and 50 degrees). If yours doesn't, your mechanic can easily file in the middle notch. I like the 37-degree notch too much to fly a Cub very long without it, because that 20-degree setting seems to produce more lift than drag; the 50-degree setting seems to do the opposite. The 37-degree notch also works well for low level survey.

Second, though the use of full flaps on takeoff is sometimes justified, the surprising thing is that a manufacturer's handbook mentions the possibility without also cautioning that the use of full flaps can be critical. The Twin Otter will take off and climb well with full flaps; and full flap takeoffs are not unusual in Cessna and Cub ski and float operations. Such operations, however, are hardly routine, and they are not talked or written about much.

The first trick in using full flaps is timing. Starting with full flaps, or applying them too early, induces too much drag and slows the initial roll. If you apply them too late in the roll, of course, you defeat their purpose. It takes practice to feel when the airplane is just about ready to fly and move to the bottom notch. The next trick, the most critical, is bleeding the flaps up to best climb. Here I question the handbook recommendation about climbing with full flaps at Vx, 45 mph. I feel that setting creates a lot of drag, and puts the plane close to stall speed, 43 mph, in any bit of unexpected turbulence or sink. Unless you have a critical situation getting over an obstacle, (which I have had), you are better off to put the nose down after breaking ground, while still in ground effect, and immediately but slowly bleed the flaps up to 37 degrees. You could go for 45, Vx, if the air is solid and stable, but you have a safer margin between Vx and Vy (which the book says is 75 mph at gross weight at sea level).

Then, when the obstacles are cleared, the remaining flaps can slowly be raised. I emphasize slowly; in a critical situation, dumping flaps suddenly will cause a momentary loss of lift you may not be able to afford, as in the doctor's scenario. Always be wary of bad air; if you get into some, raising flaps too quickly will aggravate (and add gravity!) to your problem. In other words, a third trick is, after getting off that bottom notch of flaps as soon as practical, is not to touch the 37-degree setting again until you have established a positive rate of climb **above** ground effect.

Some Terms and Ideas

The idea of adding flaps during the takeoff roll is to produce maximum lift on the wings, transferring aircraft weight from tires to wings as soon as possible. The use of flaps also decreases stall speed, allowing an airplane to fly at a lower speed.

In the Biblical story of Adam, once he had observed and named the animals, he "gained dominion" over them.

A pilot needs to be able to name certain phenomena, in that sense, in order to make good use of them. Ground Effect is the interference of the ground with the downwash field and wingtip vortices of the airfoil; hence, it goes to a height approximately equal to the wingspan. It is nice to have, as long as you understand its limits. Vx is the best angle of climb speed, 45 mph in the Cub at sea level. It is the speed that gives greatest vertical climb over a given distance. Vy is best rate of climb, listed as 75 for the Cub at sea level. It is the speed that gives greatest vertical climb during a given time. A pilot must always remember that these published speeds are at gross weight and sea level. The speeds are less as weight decreases. At the absolute ceiling of the airplane, Vy and Vx converge. The TAS for both Vy and Vx increases with altitude, of course, but Vx does so more slowly. Because of the change in TAS with altitude, the IAS for Vx and Vy eventually converge.

Most non-pilots know that a flap is some kind of quarrel or "bad scene". But every pilot should know how the skillful use of airplane flaps can help prevent a "bad scene".

Super Cubs and similar aircraft have really been modified since those early days. There are now countless STOL modifications out there, and original aircraft pilot handbooks don't mean much to those pilots and aircraft, especially when multiple mods have been incorporated. The only sensible thing for a pilot to do is practice and fly his aircraft under some semblance of a controlled environment and take some accurate notes regarding landing and takeoff distances, as well as Vx and Vy speeds, rates of climb, etc., for his particular aircraft. The good news is that performance continues to improve, and that makes operations safer for everyone.

Today, Rod Machado has a couple of great videos that explain ground effect and Vy and Vx:
https://youtu.be/0z27FAk1qtE
https://youtu.be/GHQvAQiIcoE

May 1987, Volume 5, Issue 5
Springtime Brush-Up

Instead of just boring a hole in the sky next time you head up and away, why not try a few good exercises guaranteed to sharpen you up. They won't cost you more than a few minutes, and they're worth it. First is the infamous "Dutch Roll coordination exercise." All my students hate them, and I chuckle with glee as they wallow all over the sky. I spend a few minutes of each lesson torturing them. I also use them on check rides and checkouts. I'm always amazed to find commercial pilots who never heard of them, much less know how to do them.

Actually, I still use dutch rolls myself, particularly when getting the feel of a new bird. It is a coordination exercise that develops a subconscious control touch better than any other exercise I know. They can be done at any power setting or configuration. First, set a spot on the windshield against the horizon at eye level. Then smoothly roll the airplane from side to side (I like to work to the aileron stops on the Cub), keeping the windshield spot centered absolutely. Sounds easy, eh? The urge to stop and analyze what is going on is strong but the effort is futile. The only way to do it is by seat of the pants feel, and the only way to learn it is just to wallow around the sky for a while trying it. Actually, a total of fifteen or twenty minutes is all it will take to get the idea. All three controls are used simultaneously; ailerons to roll the airplane, rudder to keep the nose centered laterally, and elevator pressure to keep the nose from rising and falling as the aircraft goes from bank to bank. The timing these constantly changing pressures is crucial, and the control touch developed while mastering this exercise is amazing. It is also of great help for crosswind procedures.

Another fun exercise is high speed taxiing. We all know the critical times with a taildragger are on the ground, and sometimes it's tempting to spend as little time as possible there. With a Cub, you don't need to spend much time on the ground, either. Try spending more time than necessary on the ground. Practice speeding up until you can get the tail up, throttle back just enough to keep it up, then bring the tail back down (throttle at idle), then repeatedly tail up, tail down, down the runway. (You need to have a quiet runway for this or a wide taxiway.)

If you feel comfortable with that, with the tail up, the next step is to run her up on one main wheel, then the other. This is excellent control practice for crosswind work. These are all procedures that my students are proficient in before they solo.

A third good practice is to do some low passes down the runway without landing, particularly in a crosswind. Concentrate on maintaining centerline with no drift (ailerons) and good rudder control to keep the nose straight. Then practice some good ole slow flight, with some turns and different flap settings.

When practicing stalls, I like to do a deep stall; power off, straight ahead, bring it to the break, then hold it there, stick full back. Get the feel of the craft in the stalled condition, walking the rudders to prevent a wing from dropping. It's a great confidence builder and lets you get to know the airplane very well in a critical flight phase.

Why do stalls, anyway? The reason is to learn to recognize, avoid, and recover from a critical flight phase. Speaking of stalls, some of the newer Cubs come with aural stalls warning horns. I think they can be useful. Granted, a lot of professionals pull the circuit breaker when doing low, slow work, because the constant noise is distracting. But on the other hand, particularly in the hands of less experienced or rusty pilots, I am convinced they could have saved some lives.

In the book "Mountain, Canyon, and Backcountry Flying" (Hoover and Williams, 2019) we describe the Dutch Roll in detail with photos. For me, it remains one of the best training maneuvers out there. Not all things change!

We had fun writing this one, as I was a dyed-in-the-wool backcountry pilot at the time. Who knew that I would end up in the corporate ranks someday! Read about that in "Notes From The Cockpit" (R.K. Williams, 2015).

June 1987, Volume 5, Issue 6
Checklists and Numbers

Cubbers are generally not "number crunchers." Number crunchers often drive high speed turboprops while wearing coats and ties. They perform weight and balance problems on fancy computers. They talk deep and slow, and never say "uh" on the radio. They fly complex aircraft that require written checklists. They are ATP rated, and what's more, instrument proficient and current. Number crunching pilots carry current Jepp charts, and they disdain VFR. The have about fifty different sets of numbers memorized, including regulation parts, V speeds, weights, tire pressures, and the boss's phone. Tailwheel airplanes, being antiques and relics of bygone days, are not among the things they think about. Their "numbers co-pilots", who don't live quite so well, fill snack cabinets and empty onboard potties. Upbeat numbers co-pilots are experts at "gear up, flaps up, shut up." Their young faces don't require a shave every day but they do have to practice saying "Yes, sir.

They sweep pebbles from underneath propellers while the captains stand by on immaculate tarmacs.

Cubbers, on the other hand (which is usually greasy), tend to wear blue jeans and t-shirts, toothpicks and baseball caps. The numbers they remember are girlfriend's telephones, beer consumption of the preceding night (approximate, honest, conservative figures), and the last three digits of their N numbers. IFR means "I follow roads, rivers, railroads, or racecars" and high-altitude flying is anything over 500'.

Having suggested the Cubbers, the flyers I am most comfortable with, take to number crunching in about the same spirit a cat takes to a bubble bath, I am about to ask my baseball-cap-wearing friends to consider a few items for memorization. When you don't have the luxury of yearly recurrent training at Flight Safety, Inc. a few standard routines and numbers could save you grief.

Checklists

During primary training, we all had checklists drummed into our heads. But, honestly, now, do you use a checklist before every takeoff and landing?

Confession time. As a flight instructor, I don't teach the use of checklists, except for check rides. Written checklists, that is. For single engine aircraft, float, ski, and wheels, I teach mental checklists. The reason is, 90 percent of the pilots I see and respect don't use written checklists. I want habit patterns to develop that will stay with a pilot for an entire flying career. Mental lists are obviously more convenient than a card you fish out of a pocket just before takeoff. Being easier to use, they will probably be used more often. As an instructor, I want to convert that "more often" to "every single cotton-pickin' time." The simple lists of CIGARS and GUMPS.

CIGARS

Cigars is for takeoff: Controls (free and correct, including flaps and water rudders), Instruments (all set and operating, including radios), Gas (quantity and tank select), Attitude (trims), run-up (mags, carb heat, prop exercise), and seatbelts (on, snub, and passenger operation and briefing).

GUMPS

Gumps is for landing: Gas (quantity and selection), Undercarriage (skis up or down, water rudder position, or amphibs position), Mixture (set for go-around, not necessarily full rich; and carb heat check). Prop (forward, or in the Cub, on and turning), and Seatbelts. Memorize and use those quick easy checklists and it's guaranteed you won't forget a potentially dangerous item.

Memorizing one more vital checklist could save your life; the five-point sequence to follow in the event of an engine failure. (1) carb heat on and fuel check (2) glide speed established (3) landing site chosen (4) restart (5) shutdown.

Most engine failures are fuel-related; hence carb heat application comes immediately, along with switching tanks. Best glide speed varies with weight, wind and altitude. The speed at sea level, no wind, at gross is 70. Lighter weight or more altitude means slower speed. A headwind calls for a slightly increased speed for penetration, while a tailwind calls for a very slightly slower speed. To establish optimum rate calls for some experimenting and watching your VSI. Best glide will generally fall between 60 and 70 mph. Remember that engine failure during climb out means an immediate decrease in angle of attack. In level or descending flight, a momentary climb to best glide speed could buy you an important couple of hundred feet, but be careful with this technique, especially close to the ground.

The choice of a place to land touches upon all kinds of variables. In practicing emergency selection, you should take account of obstructions, wind direction, slope, and time available. Restart includes checking mags, and running on one if necessary, fuel, mixture, or intentional backfire to blow carb ice. Shutdown consists of a radio call, master off, fuel off, and emergency passenger briefing.

In an actual emergency the amount of time available will dictate how far you get down the checklist. The first three; carb heat, glide speed, and landing site, can be virtually simultaneous. In actual conditions, on a takeoff engine failure at 200', you would apply carb heat, switch tanks as you lowered the nose to land straight ahead. You give a quick "I'm going down" over the radio before everything goes off, and then you concentrate on the landing.

As far as numbers to remember, best glide is between 60 and 70. Va is 93 to 96 and lowers with flaps and less weight. Vy is between 55 and 75, and Vx is between 45 and 55. All the other speeds are color-coded on the airspeed indicator. No need to strain your brain there.

Three, short five-item checklists and a couple of airspeeds to memorize. Just about anybody can steer an airplane around the sky when all is going well; the survivalist practices for "Murphy's Law" days, and becomes a pilot, not just an airplane driver. Getting the above procedures and numbers grafted into your reflexes will help your flying career, even if you don't know how to clean a port-potty and do say "uh" on the radio occasionally.

July 1987, Volume 5, Issue 7
Vital Statistics

John Robinson of Velma, Oklahoma, sent us the following articles and asked for comments:

Gates officials die in crash

Tucson, Ariz. Two senior pilots with Gates Learjet Corp. were killed Aug. 31 when the Piper Super Cub they were flying crashed shortly after takeoff from a ranch near Colorado Springs, Colo.

The pilots, aged 43 and 34, were killed in the accident, which occurred while the men were attending a meeting of top Learjet and Combs Gates personnel at a ranch owned by Harry B. Combs, a member of Learjet's board of directors. The ranch is located about 25 miles northeast of Colorado Springs, and the 1974 model aircraft involved in the accident, N41331, was registered to Combs.

One of the pilots was the chief of production test flight for the company. The other was director of flight operations for Combs Gates in Denver.

Investigators say the flight began about 3:30 p.m. MDT after the two men decided to take a pleasure flight because one of them had never flown in a Super Cub.

The aircraft lifted off about halfway down the 3640' dirt strip. The plane then began a steep left turn and started to sideslip to the left when it had reached a point about two-thirds of the way down the runway and an altitude of about 200', according to witnesses.

Witnesses said the aircraft appeared to recover

briefly before it side slipped to the right and crashed and burned.

The ranch's landing strip is at an elevation of 6540' and the temperature at the time of the crash was 91 degrees.

When Jim talked to the NTSB investigator he got some additional information. The pilots were more experienced in Learjets than in Cubs, there was no known malfunction of the aircraft, both men weighted over 200 pounds, the density altitude was 9000', and the airplane entered a 60-degree left bank at 50 to 200'AGL.

So, without reflecting on the knowledge or skills of the deceased fliers, or playing the game of private investigator, every serious pilot who looks at an accident report can't help asking, "If I had been there what would have happened?" Let's assume two things. (1) On behalf of the individuals involved, we will assume that there were unavoidable unknowns in this particular tragedy. (2) But on behalf of the living we will look at similar general factors in the light of certain "vital statistics"—data that can make a life or death difference for each one of us.

First, let's really look at the density altitude factor. A vital performance rule of thumb is that for every 1000' of density altitude, the airplane will take about 8.5% longer takeoff run. An airplane that rolls 400' at sea level density altitude will require, at 9000', a ground roll of about 700', almost twice the distance. That alone may have surprised the pilots some.

Let's look at another vital formula. The power to weight ratio of a 150 horsepower Cub is 11.6 (1750 pounds divided by 150). This good ratio has a lot to do with what makes a Super Cub "super." But what kind of power to weight ratio will you have when you transport our Super Cub to a scene similar to that of the accident? At sea level, you theoretically have 30" manifold pressure, and lose one inch for every thousand feet of density altitude (d.a.). thus, at 9000' 30-9=21" of m.p.

Every inch of manifold pressure represents five horsepower (150 divided by 30" =5 hp); so, 5 x 21 = 105 HP.

With that horsepower, the power to weight ratio is far higher: 1750 divided by 105 = 16.6 power/weight ratio. Imagine the loss of climb performance in those circumstances! It might have surprised them if they hadn't thought about it beforehand.

In other words, if we were flying at the Combs ranch in 90-degree weather, our Super Cub would not even be close to a 11.6 power/weight ratio, and its horsepower would not be 150, but 105. If the two of us 200 pounders had coaxed a 150 HP performance out of the plane, given these circumstances, we would have magically reduced the gross weight by 532 pounds! An excellent airplane is not a flying carpet, and you can't expect it to repeal the laws of physics.

Can "pilot attitude" also make a difference? Well, suppose your flying habits were associated with the older Learjets, which, like the model 24s, behave like a military fighter. They will climb 6000 feet per minute on one engine, I'm told. Suppose you, a seasoned Lear pilot, had told your buddy about the Cub's superior STOL characteristics, and wanted to demonstrate them. Maybe you wanted more impressive performance than the Lear's.

You wouldn't get it. The Super Cub, a great airplane, is not a helicopter, not a Lear jet, not a flying carpet. It obeys the laws of aerodynamics and gravity.

If you somehow failed to allow for hostile performance—weakening factors, you could easily stall your Cub on climb out—an accelerated stall if you made a steep left bank. You might experience a secondary stall during your attempted recovery. If you failed to lower the nose to break the stall, and tried to power out of it, you could lose a nice airplane, and maybe your life. Maybe you can power your way out of an incipient Learjet stall, but it doesn't work in a Cub. Just because a Cub is small, light, and simple, you can't safely assume that it flies the same way everywhere, or that it flies like the plane you're used to.

One great difference between an aviation career today and career in Lindbergh's time is that today you have to specialize. As a professional you must decide whether you want military or commercial, airline or air taxi, bush or instrument, heavy aircraft or light, and on and on. A 747 jock develops habits that work to his disadvantage in a Cub or in flying backcountry air taxi. And vice versa. The unfortunate pilots in many an accident have been experts in equipment quite different from what they crashed in.

Every pilot wants to grow in flexibility, competence, and dependability. And the determined survivalist knows that flying a new type of aircraft means more than acquiring new skills—you have to live by new attitudes and date banks as well. Occasionally—not often, I'm thankful to say—your only alternative may lie between becoming and applying vital statistics.

Ironically, I ended up with thousands of hours in Learjets. And my son flies the F-22 Raptor. He was once asked how he transitioned from the Raptor to the Cub. His answer: "They are at such polar opposites that there is no transference." Interestingly, though, he still claims to relate basic mental fundamentals to both.

August 1987, Volume 5, Issue 8
Power Curves

The back side of the power curve, or the "area of reverse command," is much talked about in STOL procedures. When a reduction in airspeed brings about the need for increased power if altitude is to be maintained, you are on the back side. This is also called "mushing" or "hanging on the prop." Drag is greater than thrust. On some underpowered airplanes, even full throttle will not make the craft climb or accelerate. More power is required to recover. After full power is used, a sacrifice in altitude is the only option. In other words, increased power, airspeed, or both will be necessary to get back on the front side. Low airspeed and high angle of attack are clues that you are near or in the area of reverse command.

The power curve is also related to the infamous argument of what controls airspeed and altitude, throttle or elevator. Sparky Imeson has the best way of saying it: "On the back side of the power curve, control airspeed with elevator, altitude with throttle. On the front side, airspeed control is with throttle, altitude is controlled with elevator." There is still another way of explaining how to cope with the power curve. When you are on the front side, the aircraft will be inherently stable, returning to its original airspeed after induced fluctuation. On the back side, the plane may not display the same docile characteristics.

In STOL operations, flying behind the power curve can be fairly routine. It is such a critical phase of flight, however, that the pilot must understand what is happening. A steeper approach (glideslope-wise) is one way to operate behind the power curve on landing. Then you are not trying to maintain altitude but are flying a stabilized power-on approach. Keep in mind the pitch attitude and angle of attack are rarely the same. Pitch attitude is the angle of the airplane relative to the ground, or the sight picture over the nose, while angle of attack is the angle of the wing relative to the flight path of the airplane. In a power-on approach behind the power curve the runway should be in sight over the nose to keep the angle of attack lower. And you have altitude to sacrifice if you need to come back towards the front side of the curve. In a low, slow, flatter glide slope approach flown at a higher angle of attack and pitch attitude your options are less, unless you have the ability and power to throttle your way through to the front side.

Some aircraft are obviously more of a handful behind the power curve than others. A Cessna 207 or 150, at gross, for example, is an unforgettable experience on the back side. On the other end of the scale, a Super Cub, particularly with the Borer prop, is more difficult to get in trouble with. The area of reverse command, however, is still something to be prepared for. With full flaps, gross weight and at high density altitudes, "play with" (viz., extend your mastery of) your particular airplane. Try an airspeed around 45 or 50, hold altitude, then slow down while maintaining altitude. When you need to increase power to maintain that altitude, you are behind the power curve. Then see how slow you can go, with full power, without losing altitude (be careful of the stall). Now you will see what a performer the Cub is. In most situations, enough power is available to force the craft to accelerate without losing altitude, and with full power it is almost impossible to fall behind the power curve. Command reversal has happened, however, with Super Cubs. In a marginal takeoff or in a slow, flat approach, high density altitude, sinking air, and heavy loads can bite you when there's no time or space to recover. Avoid such surprises. Practice at altitude and learn your airplane.

We still see today, over and over again, that practice is the key to sharpness.

September 1987, Volume 5, Issue 9
Give Yourself a Brake

Before you head for that secret hunting spot this fall, a little study of your Cub brakes is recommended, followed by some preventive maintenance. I reinforce the point with a story of one of my first Cub trips into the wilderness, to Running Creek in the Selway Bitterroot Wilderness. The approach end of the ten percent graded dirt strip meets the Selway River.

The owner then, and hero of this anecdote, was a likeable chap who had forgotten more about aviation than most pilots can ever hope to learn: George Madsen, a former test pilot and test pilot instructor in the air Force. He had retired to the Selway with a beautiful 185. Incredibly, to climb out through the infamous Selway fog, he had his own instrument departure, plate and all. Quite an experience, it was, to be hunting up on a ridge, looking down on a solid blanket of fog on the river, and suddenly hear an airplane roar to life and eventually pop up through the white and into the blue. But the present anecdote doesn't concern George's 185.

On the perfect morning I tried out Running Creek, there was no fog or wind. Nice landing, too. The problem developed during the taxi back downhill toward the river. I touched the brakes and felt the familiar next to nothing, followed by a total nothing. I pulled the mixture as we began accelerating toward the water and hollered at my passenger to try his brakes. He slowed us down a little before reporting no more pedal.

The strip was lined with six to eight-inch logs and

an electric wire fence. I held the stick full back and hit left rudder. We hoped the log wouldn't flip us over (the Cub had stock wheels and brakes). It didn't.

The next problem was explaining the situation to George, who was on his way up from the lodge. He seemed more amused than anything. I introduced myself and explained the predicament. No problem, George said; he had brake fluid in the shed. We pushed the Cub back onto the airstrip and were trying to reconstruct some electric fencing when George returned with wrenches and fluid. I had to humble myself further by admitting I had no idea where the brake cylinders were, or how to service them. He graciously showed me the "old Alaskan way" to service Cub brakes: set the parking brakes and fill the cylinders from the top (which are under the front seat, by the way).

I don't believe anyone has ever been overawed by Super Cub brakes, which are rarely needed anyway, because of the Cub's low landing speeds. But get in a situation like the one I had at Running Creek, or land hot because of a screw up or a tailwind gust, or any number of unexpected, and you will instantly crave more. Sports car racers understand and live by an adage my uncle taught me: the go power mustn't overmatch handling and the whoa power. In other words, get the best brakes you can.

Of the several ways to handle the problem, none I know of will be a complete fix. Smaller tires will improve braking, as will the Cleveland wheel and disc brake conversion. The STC'd replacement cylinders have been disappointing to me, although others seem happy with them. The toe brake conversion may be a good solution, but I haven't tried it because it goes too far toward bastardizing the airplane. Some pilots with tundra tires will top the cylinders before a trip to a very short field, using the technique mentioned earlier, and then let some fluid out for take-off to eliminate the wheel drag. Super Cub brakes are not perfect, even the de-Piperized ones. They are usually not a serious problem, but something to be aware of and plan for. If I'm going somewhere I need to count on brakes, they are a major preflight item.

My mechanic, Lenny Skunberg of Lenny's Airmotive in Salmon, Idaho, just won the General Aviation Maintenance Technician of the Year Award and will be in Washington, D.C. the week of October 12 to receive gifts and awards. Besides giving me a chance to brag about a friend, this news offers a good excuse to talk about choosing a safe mechanic. The choice is yours, and it is important. Does your mechanic have a good reputation? Does he specialize in the right areas (dope and fabric, Lycoming, Super Cubs)? Does he use a checklist? Does he have a current AD list for your aircraft? Does he let you help, or at least watch? Does he keep you legal? Does he try to save you money without cutting corners? Does he double and triple check his work? A good mechanic is worth traveling a long, long way for. One friend of mine purposefully changes mechanics periodically on the theory that a fresh mind and eye may pick up something not noticed before.

It pays to take a direct interest in the maintenance of your airplane. Structural and engine failure are on the low end of accident cause but cannot be ignored. Get involved in maintenance.

Today almost no one uses the original Scott brake cylinders on Cubs. There are several excellent after-market substitutes. Remember that large tires decrease brake effectiveness.

October 1987, Volume 5, Issue 10
Three Shots at the Wind

One beautiful spring day, with not a hint of wind, we flew to south Idaho to visit in-laws. When we located my father-in-law working in a field we landed nearby on a sage covered hill with an old jeep track on it. Even though conditions were perfect, I used my tie down kit. Joe drove up in the truck and took us to the house for dinner. I could see the Cub from the back window, a couple of miles away.

As we were finishing up dinner, the wind began to come up. I needed gas in nearby Buhl anyway, so we went to get the Cub. By the time we got there it was blowing fifteen to twenty mph, enough to warrant a take-off uphill. As I popped up over the hill the windstorm became visible as a line of dust to the west. After the short trip to Buhl the wind was blowing about twenty to twenty-five, right down the runway. I taxied to the pumps, parked into the wind, and made the nearly disastrous decision to get fuel while waiting for my father-in-law to arrive in the pickup. The airport manager was in his mobile home, demobilized by a full leg cast. I got the gas key and had the left tank almost full when the windstorm hit.

There was no question that I had an immediate and serious problem. I threw the gas hose down, jumped off the ladder, and hung on to the left-wing strut. The wind had probably reached forty to forty-five by then, and the tires were very light on the ground, the wings taking most of the aircraft weight in preparation for flight, manned or otherwise.

My father-in-law arrived in the proverbial nick of time. With the wind up to at least fifty to sixty mph, no words between us were necessary, or possible. There was too much noise. He jumped from the pickup to grab the other wing strut. Within seconds the left tire lifted off the ground about eight inches, and the right came up at least two or three. I thought my Cub's number was up. I could visualize it tumbling over backwards into the C-150 behind and then into the office building beyond. Desperate, convinced that any second the wind would flip the plane away from us (or flip it with us), we were at a loss to do anything but hang on. We couldn't talk, couldn't see. Our eyes, ears, and pockets filled with grit.

Finally, the airport manager hobbled outside and into a gas truck which he drove in front of the airplane. That windbreak helped significantly. After we had hung on to the Cub for a long forty-five minutes, the storm abated slightly. Eventually I was able to crawl inside the bird while they tied it to the truck. The worst was over. After the tie down, we heaved sighs of relief and stood around for a while, drained, thinking about what had happened.

You will not find it hard to believe that I was feeling stupid. There was no excuse for not having gone directly to the tie-downs after landing. After making a serious mistake I had re-learned a lesson the hard way, in a painful laboratory "exercise:" don't mess with Mother Wind. And, more specifically, point one: never neglect the tie down. It's a sacred ritual.

Mother Wind is, among other things, treacherous and unpredictable. I found that out many years earlier, sailing through the South Pacific; I had been in the awkward position of understanding the wind's perfidious nature, yet having to rely on it for transportation. The problems are likely to be even more critical in an airplane than in a sailboat, especially in a machine as light as the Cub is. What completely convinced me of the latter point was flying a Cub through the Grand Tetons from east to west, with the wind blowing about forty knots. I was holding on for dear life, swearing that if both wings stayed attached, and if the plane made it, and if I ever got another chance, I would be wiser next time, and go around. I expect to keep that resolution, which is point two in today's column: Anticipate wind patterns and avoid idiotic flight plans. Cub drivers need to remember that a thousand-pound airplane that will fly at 30 mph is very susceptible. I saw a great sign the other day that belongs on the panel of my Cub in plain sight, and I'm going to find one and put it there. It pleads, "Don't Do Anything Stupid."

Wind during the touchdown is the worst in-flight scenario. In the canyons, an easy approach to an easy landing can be quickly changed to riding the limit of control. And wind can make an already difficult landing impossible to manage without damage unless you have help from another famously unreliable source, Lady Luck. In a Pawnee once, in a crosswind, I was befriended by her. The touchdown was good, but on the rollout, with the tail still up, the plane encountered some bad air turning silly as it raced through a row of hangars. Control was marginal for a few seconds, and the lessons of those few seconds have lasted for a few years. Don't quit flying until you are completely stopped.

In the Cub, last spring, I had been allowing a passenger in the back seat to practice some landings, full stall. There had been no problems. The wind felt solid, right down the runway. When he was a little high on one approach I gave him full flaps, a move which happened to increase our vulnerability at a crucial moment, because of less aileron control. As he touched with a slight bounce, the wind took a sudden wild 45-degree swing to the right. The left wingtip came down to the ground, bringing the right tire off. There had been no warning. I yelled, "I got it!" and simultaneously jammed full power and full right forward stick. We hung there for a second or two, balanced between the wind and 150 Lycoming horses. This time, Lycoming, Borer, Piper, and Williams won out, and the Cub righted. All four of us were shaking when we stopped.

The student and I didn't think we had actually touched the wingtip until an inspection revealed some scraped fabric that would require minor cosmetic repairs.

Those landings tend to make you remember the old saw about ground-looping: "There're those who have, and there are those who will." I still don't concede that a ground loop is inevitable in my future. But that squirrelly, unpredictable wind that tried to eat me about every three thousand hours brings me back to point three, recognizing that the wind is more treacherous and craftier than I, and bigger and stronger than my Super Cub: In landing especially, try to be ready for instant hostility from the wind.

Last month's question was: An airplane takes off with one thousand pounds of cargo, canaries in cages. The canaries weight 100 pounds and the cages weigh 900 pounds. Total takeoff weight is three thousand pounds. During the trip, all the canaries simultaneously start flying inside their cages. How much does the airplane weight during this time?

The answer: Your airplane will weigh the same whether or not the canaries are flying. Their wings are supporting their weight, but the downforce of air the wings produce is equal to the weight of the canaries.

So the weight inside, or payload, stays the same. This one was a little hard for us to be sure of, but we checked with a physics professor at the local university to verify.

November 1987, Volume 5, Issue 11
The Wind Doesn't Blow, It Sucks

Three fatalities, two wrecked airplanes, one damaged craft and ego, all since the last issue.

Wind.

Of course, it's inaccurate and unfair to blame one element for an accident or incident. They are almost always the result of a series of poor judgment, multiple emergencies, or both.

The first accident involved a Super Cub doing a buzz job near a reservoir in about 20 knots of wind. On his second pass he clipped a camper's tent, a car, and then went into the reservoir. His passenger perished. The campers were the passenger's parents. They watched their son drown.

The second was a Luscombe. An acquaintance of mine, in a canyon in the Sierras, in a strong wind, whose last transmission to two other Luscombes above him was something like, "You guys don't want to get down in here."

The third was a friend with a new Cub at his home strip. Alone in the front, taxiing, he turned downhill, downwind, power at idle with the stick all the way back. He nosed over.

All of these problems were at least partially caused by the wind. All were avoidable. The first, perhaps was idiotic and suicidal. The second, maybe, caused by inexperience and lack of staying ahead of the airplane, with the knowledge he was in trouble. The last the result of complacency and forgetting lessons learned long ago, having been flying heavier airplanes (this one was probably avoidable just by having the stick forward as he turned downhill and downwind—remember your basic stick positions in regard to wind direction?).

We've discussed wind quite a bit in this newsletter, and probably will continue to. We know it is our #1 enemy (except when lucky people like Jim find 50 knot tailwinds going cross-country!).

So, what are we supposed to do about it? Park it in the barn whenever it decides to blow, or because it looks like it might blow?

First of all, we need to get and stay as competent in the wind as we can. Be comfortable in a crosswind, know how to taxi in the wind, and get some good dual if we're rusty. And be aware of how it affects us enroute, with downdrafts, airframe stress, and controllability.

Next, after we are current, knowledgeable, and competent, we need to have a working set of limits.

It is sometimes a revelation to learn how often the pros say "no". They say it on a regular basic.

There is terrain I won't hunt coyotes in in certain wind conditions. There is wind I won't taxi in without wing walkers. There is canyon wind I won't land a Twin Otter in, much less a Super Cub. There are winds aloft that I won't fly over the mountains in a Cub.

It's the guys with the big yellow stripes who have nothing to prove that stay alive. It's the pilots who "can always handle it" who get hurt.

We need to be good, competent pilots in the wind. But we need to know our limits and when to say "no" to the wind.

Remember, to any pilot, but particularly to the light

tailwheel airplane pilot, the wind doesn't blow; it sucks!

I still hate the wind when it comes to Super Cub flying. The craft is so light, with light wing-loading, that it is easy to feel out of control in high winds aloft. With Cessna 182s on up, I don't care nearly as much, but these days I fly for fun, and flying over mountains with wind and the accompanying turbulence just takes the fun out of it.

December 1987, Volume 5, Issue 12
Night Flight

When it's good, it's great. When it's bad, it's terrible. Night flying, that is. It provided one of my "Never Again" experiences. The unfamiliar airplane involved was a Piper, a twin-engine model. About one a.m., after an evening concert in Spokane, I was flying the boss and some friends of his back to Salmon, Idaho. I was tired. The weather was IFR enroute with stars shining overhead Salmon. The boss assured us we had plenty of fuel to get home, and I foolishly believed him. He had had more time in the plane than I did, it was only my third flight in that model, and, after all, he was the boss.

We realized enroute that fuel would be an issue. Not really critical, we would have legal reserves after going to economy cruise. But considering Salmon's location and distance from an alternate, and no instrument approaches, "legal reserves" were way below practical safety limits. The fuel system on this aircraft, a Navajo Chieftain, is fairly complex: four tanks, multiple cross-feeds. The flight was smooth, with no ice, but more and more nerve-wracking as we approached Salmon. There wasn't much gas, and the clear sky promised us was a long time coming. We were right on top of town before finally breaking out.

When we went visual, I started descending circles to the left, coming down from twelve thousand feet. On a long descent, when a pilot needs to keep engine temperatures up, one solution is to leave the mixtures lean. As I entered downwind I added power to stop the descent. Nothing happened. More power. Still nothing. Again, more power, this time producing quite discouraging engine coughs and sputters. All six engine controls went forward, the standard emergency response. My heart skipped, but when the mixtures came forward, the engines surged and ran. I had starved them during the descent, because in the darkness the mixture controls, out of sight, were also out of mind.

As I recovered from that fright (by this time I had completed a 180 and was set up for a downwind on the opposite runway), the left engine suddenly began to surge, trying to quit, then catching again. I checked the boost pumps and switched tanks. My boss was screaming, "Feather it! Feather it!" I was rattled but shook my head. "No, it's still developing some power. There's a fuel problem."

The engine began running smoothly on base, but by that time I was powered back and had the runway made. I realized, after landing and gaining control of the shakes, that I had starved the left engine from fuel while in the long circling descent.

This was, for the most part, a night induced problem. Granted, I was also tired, had poor weather, and was unfamiliar with the aircraft—a good accident producing combination. But there was another factor still, a deadly tendency pilots know about theoretically, and often forget under pressure: In night flying, as in instrument flying, it's all too easy to fixate on one or two things. Practice and a good instructor will eventually correct that tendency and develop good scanning habits. The need to overcome natural tendencies makes night flying a special skill. Proficiency requires more training than three hours and ten landings as a student pilot.

In one sense, night flying is actually harder than instruments, because the pilot is constantly moving from outside to inside, which is the most dangerous and difficult time on instrument flight. I believe that in a similar situation in daylight, my chances of running a tank dry would be much less than at night, just because things like fuel selectors are easier to see in daylight.

The pilot's options are limited in night flying. Dark is okay if fuel and weather are fine. Take away either the fuel or weather reserve and it gets dicey. Take away both and it's just a matter of time before you get bitten, hard. A safe landing after engine failure, of course, becomes a matter of luck, even if you know the terrain. Some pilots consider it prudent to follow roads or more populated routes over mountains. Navigation is easier and you do have more options after an engine failure. Roads become good landing sites, except for power lines and traffic. The pros who travel the same routes memorize good landing spots and wire locations. We made a point of this in the sailplane flying business, where off field landings were always a possibility.

On a dark night with no moon, flying gets a little tough in the average VFR Cub. Most ATPs I know would rather not have to go needle, ball, and airspeed at any time, but that's about what you're doing on a dark night without instruments.

For me, a horizon must be visible if I can't go from city lights to city lights in flat terrain. Radio navigation becomes more important at night. Pilotage and dead reckoning are harder. It's easy to forget checklist items in the dark, where they can't be seen. Blind cockpit checks are good practice for night flying. Sit in there with your eyes closed and be able to find everything-gauges, controls, and switches-by feel only.

I often used to fly at night between Boise and Salmon, when the weather was good, and I mean very good, with no clouds under 12 to 15 thousand feet. But I lost my enthusiasm for that dark mountainous route after things kept going wrong with the company-owned aircraft I was flying. One time after a vacuum pump failure the gyros failed. Another time, the interior lights said goodbye; next, the landing lights. Nothing really major, mind you, but enough to take notice of. It seemed maybe Someone was telling me something. I was never good at taking brush-off hints from possible girlfriends, and they had to get pretty blunt about it before I would get the picture. But as a pilot, I have learned to take a hint early on, to know that the airplane is always talking to you in its own language. Intuition is an important part of safe flying.

There is a plus side to night flying. Some of the best flights I have ever had have been at night, with a beautiful clear sky, smooth air, light traffic (and what is out is easier to see), and easy navigation, with cities visible for scores of miles. Not a thing in the world wrong with it, I think, as long as the limits are set correctly, and you Don't Do Anything Stupid (like fixating on half your checklist).

Last month's question: You are unfortunate enough to go IFR with no gyros or instruments, but you know there are no obstacles in any direction. Which direction is it safest to go? (Assume you don't know where VFR weather or anything else is and are steering by the magnetic compass). The answer is to fly a heading of south. The magnetic compass has fewer errors on this heading than any other. That was a question the FAA gave me on my Glider Instructor check ride. Good grief, how does that apply to sailplane flying?

January 1988, Volume 6, Issue 1
Schussing Part I

Schussing? Well, not exactly, but skiing, nonetheless. The season for it has arrived, for great fun in a Super Cub, and for occasional hard work in, say, a Cessna 185 wearing Fluidyne 4000 hydraulic skis.

I want to tell you about a couple of ski runs to Cold Meadows. You've read about Cold Meadows in this column before, one of the longer and better airstrips in the Idaho Wilderness. Why is it such a spot for action and excitement? The first trip, the one I will describe this month, was in a 185, on a squally, windy afternoon in later November. I was taking supplies in to a hunting camp and hauling more gear out. With the season ending, no "dudes" were around, just the guides.

To find a path into the Meadows, against terrific headwinds, I had to try three different routes, and the combined weight and drag of skis had slowed the aircraft fifteen to twenty mph. Consequently, the fuel burn was quite a lot higher than anticipated. The approach and landing were routine. Landing checklists, however, are crucial with retract skis. My former boss once forgot to put gear down (skis) and only with the help of strong bungees and the grace of God stayed upright on touchdown.

Given the use of a checklist, though, (GUMPS), and the powder conditions common in Idaho, ski landings are generally a piece of cake, smooth and light. On ice or hard pack stopping can be a major problem, and about all one can do is use the tailwheel or leave the skis up. I like wheel landings, so the speed can stay up in powder and I can feel out the snow conditions better.

After our landing a big squall moved in and nailed us with another two inches of snow. It was too late to go home by the time the storm had passed, so we covered the wings and windshield with packing manties, raised the skis with blocks under the tires and scraped the ski bottoms clean. We had to do that to keep them from freezing to the surface, otherwise they will stick hard to the ground, even after a few minutes. The friction from landing warms the bottoms, which melt the surface snow. The water below the skis then cools and freezes onto the ski bottoms.

Our lodging was surprisingly comfortable, for being an outfitter's tent in the wilderness at 6800' in three and a half feet of snow. Over the course of the next three days and two nights I even made a little money, about $1.75 playing penny ante poker with the guides. We had radio contact with my home base, which kept the search party relaxed and grounded. The weather, though, was miserable; it snowed off and on with no real letup, producing about twelve inches more during our little vacation. I had to spend about five hours a day on snowshoes, packing the strip. I used the airplane some, to keep it warmed up, but the full power runs necessary to keep the plane moving to pack the snow would burn fuel we couldn't afford. And turning the thing around at the end of the strip was always a tiring two or three-man job.

When I finally did get out, it was after several take off attempts and subsequent down loadings, and a stop at another airstrip for more gas before heading home. Looking back, we all thought it was a fun and safe adventure, but one that left us exhausted after it was over.

It entailed much of the bad about ski flying, and besides demonstrating how tiring and time-consuming the whole process can be, it serves as a reminder of the importance of attention to survival equipment.

On another subject, George Cavies wrote in asking for more information on the subject of airspeed and altitude control with throttle and elevator. As a sailplane pilot, George has the best possible background for mountain and canyon flying. In a sailplane, of course, since there is no throttle, airspeed must be controlled by elevator.

To clarify this principle, pretend that we are IFR in our sailplane and ATC gives this clearance: "Maintain 6000' and 100 knots." What controls airspeed? Elevator, right? Hmmm. Let's go back to the concept of the power curve as a means of describing various flight situations: "When a reduction in airspeed brings about the need for increased power if altitude is to be maintained, you are on the back side of the power curve."

When the sailplane levels off and slows to 100 knots, some source of power will be needed to maintain an altitude of 6000'. We have no choice. Elevator controls both airspeed and altitude, until minimum glide speed is met; then elevator controls airspeed and you look for lift to control altitude.

That's where an engine changes the picture. "Maintain 6000' and 100 knots." Now what is going to control airspeed, after you've leveled off at 6000'? Throttle. It has to be. If you used elevator, you could not maintain 6000'. The aircraft is working towards the back side of the power curve, something a sailplane cannot do.

However, the important thing to remember, as George says, is that during the critical phases of flight, takeoff and landing, the elevator must control airspeed. If you're thinking the other way, and have engine failure, you are in a world of hurt. Set elevator pitch for the airspeed you want, and engine power to the altitude you want, both up or down. If you just want to concentrate on the critical flight phases, takeoffs and landings, VFR, remember: airspeed-elevator; altitude-throttle. Too bad there isn't one simple formula for all flight phases, or a simple answer to George's question. Maybe you don't want to think about flying a glide slope IFR. It becomes more complicated as both throttle and elevator control airspeed and vertical speed together, with throttle primarily controlling speed and elevator primarily controlling descent.

Last month's question: What are the five left-turning tendencies in an airplane? The four commonly recognized influences are torque, gyroscopic precession and P factor, and corkscrew effect (now more commonly called spiraling slipstream). Briefly, torque is caused by the crankshaft turning clockwise as seen from the cockpit, delivering horsepower in that direction. Gyroscopic precession takes place when the propeller axis is tilted with the tail coming up, and changes the direction of the propeller's force, which is a forward force on the right side, 90 degrees ahead in the direction of rotation, pulling the nose left. P factor is somewhat similar and often combined with precession. As angle of attack is increased, the down moving propeller blade has a greater bite than the up moving blade, because it meets the relative wind at a greater angle of attack.

This increased thrust causes a yaw to the left. The fourth influence, the corkscrew effect, is caused by the prop blast circling around under the fuselage and hitting the rudder on the side, pushing the tail right and nose left.

The kicker, if you're still with me, is the left main tire, the fifth left turn inducer. The added weight on the left tire caused by the above-named elements will also cause the aircraft to pull left, adding another little known (and perhaps, by now, little cared about) left turning tendency. This effect is even more noticeable with today's large bush tires.

For this month's little hummer: You are on a two-way E-W (either direction) airstrip, with a 90-degree crosswind coming out of the north. Which is the best way to take off, for the shortest ground roll?

February 1988, Volume 6, Issue 2
Schussing, Part II

Last month I told you about a prolonged ski run to Cold Meadows. We were in a Cessna 185, caught by bad weather, and took an unscheduled three-day vacation. I've been saving a second report, on a run I enjoyed a lot more, for this month. The trip, which covered approximately the same route, was in a Super Cub, and it was great. In the middle of the wilderness on a cold, clear blue-sky day, the beauty, stillness, and isolation can be breathtaking. The Cub really shows its colors as a ski plane. It doesn't easily get bogged down in powder, and it's easy to maneuver. Stinson, 185s, 180s, and other heavier airplanes cannot say the same.

On that second trip, I was heavy with a passenger and survival gear, and the snow was about four feet of powder, about half of it packed. I had a tail ski on but it wasn't needed (it might be with the third seat at max, however). On a Cub, the tail comes up beautifully, and we never had to get out to turn around. It was so easy! For fun I tried taking off in fresh snow, rather than my landing tracks. Terminal velocity seemed to be about fifteen to twenty mph. But when I slid over into my one landing tracks, the plane performed as though it had its old rubber shoes back on grass.

Besides being much lighter than a Cessna, the Super Cub had wheel replacement skis, not hydraulics. Simpler and more fun. The one annoying detail is that one should have snow to land on. It's easier on the bottoms. I have Aeroski 3000s for my Cub right now, and they are fantastic. Teflon bottoms are good, but the plastic ones are best. Outfit your plane, pick some good weather, find an instructor if you can, and go try it out. I highly recommend the pleasure and thrill of skiing in a Super Cub.

A few tips might be helpful. Preflight must be more involved. The pilot should check all hydraulic lines and fittings, cables, attach point, axle clips, ski bottoms, wheel clearance, springs, bungees, wax, tool kit, snowshoes, and survival gear. Especially with hydraulic skis, plan longer takeoffs, slower climbs, slower cruise, and higher fuel burn. Pay attention to which category your skis put your plane in, utility or normal. Not that you would want to do spins with skis on!

If you have had practice in a heavy airplane with hydraulic skis, of course, and can make the necessary moves, your Super Cub will feel like a plaything. About the only advantage you lose is the ability to land on dry surfaces. The chief problems are turning and takeoffs. Let's look at those two maneuvers.

In making a turn, unless you have acres to move in, or have extra manpower (weightlifters preferred) back by the tail pushing and kicking the tailwheel while you are blasting with the power and jumping up and down in the seat to break the skis loose, the procedure goes something like this:

For torque assistance, plan for left turns, in which the left wheel and right ski will be on the surface. The right hand operates the pump handle, and sometimes the throttle. Push left rudder and right brake (to hold the right ski down and left ski up) as you pump madly on the handle. If you're an accomplished contortionist, keep the tail up with the stick at the same time If you have a lot of luck and good timing, the tail will not bog down in the unpacked powder and the craft will pivot around the lowered left tire.

Next, with the airplane lined up on the runway, pump the left ski back down. By this time, regardless of the temperature, you are definitely sweating. Caution must be used not to turn too sharply. Too sharp a turn can dig in the right ski and cause side stress on the gear, or even spring or fold it. But turn too slowly, and your momentum won't be enough to carry the plane through the turn. Add a grade and add a marginal turning radius arc (such as the Cold Meadows strip, or worse), and things get downright tricky. I figure I'm pretty lucky any time I can turn a ski plane around without having to get out at least once to push, dig, and kick.

Now comes the fun part. Take off. The good news about powder is that aborting the takeoff and stopping is generally not a problem. The bad news is that aborting in powder becomes almost routine. Determining the liftoff point is critical. In deciding where it is, consider climb out and terrain obstacles, and also the extra drag of the skis and the snow they may be carrying. The technique is very similar to floatplane flying. In a standard three-point soft field takeoff, often the bird will reach a terminal velocity well below liftoff speed. As a result, the craft simply drives on down the runway without gaining any speed. So, the first thing is to get the tail up. Nosing over is not much of a threat with skis, unless you hit a large drift. Don't get the tail way up, just out of the snow. This also leaves the wing at a better angle of attack for climb. This is similar to getting a floatplane on the step. Next, when the ailerons get effective, lift a ski up. The ski bottoms, like floats, can create a suction between themselves and the snow, and that suction must be broken to have a prayer of lifting off. Light to moderate bouncing with the elevator control can also help. All this time directional control must be maintained, feeling for the plane's responsiveness and lightness, and watching for the go/no-go spot. If it comes, and the airplane isn't on its way loose, it's time to throttle back and settle in.

Then it's back to turning around, downloading, and/or packing the strip some more.

Bill Dorris of McCall Air Taxi is one of the most experienced ski fliers in Idaho. He told me once about a takeoff from Cold Meadows in a 185 on hydraulic skis: "The snow conditions were just awful. I kept downloading and downloading until I had just one hunting guide and his hat. And after we finally got off, I was wishing he had left his hat."

Float pilots know that sometimes full flaps are needed to break loose from the water. Again, it holds true for skis. The added flaps help transfer aircraft weight from gear to wings, and that's what you want. Even if full flaps are creating more drag than lift, the plane will fly slower with them and break loose easier. Practicing full flap takeoffs on wheels and getting the timing down makes for an easier transition to skis. Many times, ski takeoffs are just not possible without full flaps. Being able to work flaps manually helps a great deal, another reason Cubs and 185s are so popular with the bush crowd.

Immediately after breaking ground, the flaps

must be bled up slowly to best climb setting as the nose is lowered. Then pump those skis up. Most craft climb better with the skis retracted, and this can be crucial if obstacles stand ahead.

Last month's question was about direction of takeoff with a direct crosswind. The answer is you should take off with the wind coming from right to left, which in the example would mean taking off to the west. The airplane will want to weathervane into the wind or turn right. This will counteract the built-in left turning tendency and cancel them out to some degree. This in turn means that there will be less rudder sticking out in the slipstream, which means less drag and a shorter ground roll.

Spring 1988, Volume 6, Issue 3
(Beginning with this issue dates were not included)
Microbursts

Luckily, the record reads "No accidents, no violations", but unfortunately, my flying history doesn't exclude "incidents". That occurred on my birthday, August 5, 1979, at the peak of the whitewater boating season in the wilderness area of Idaho. Low river water levels had the backcountry air taxi companies really humping. The raging Mortar Creek fire had consumed 65,000 acres, closing the upper Middle Fork of the Salmon to both boating and flying. Visibility in the canyon was right down to one-mile minimums, with heavy smoke in places. The air taxis were still flying boaters in to the shorter airstrips downstream.

Even though the company I worked for had seven pilots going, my share of flying in July had been well over 200 hours, all short hops into the canyons, at gross weight. Our chief pilot had a roaring hangover the morning of August 5 and rescheduled us to accommodate his head. His new plan put me flying five late morning passengers in a 207 to Simplot, a 900-foot one-way strip at 4,000' elevation. Those conditions weren't ideal, but acceptable.

After the usual delays, it was just a few minutes before noon as I circled the airstrip. It wasn't too hot yet, and the smoke in the canyon wasn't at its thickest. But as I circled, the windsock took a pull out of the southwest. The wind current lasted only a few seconds, and the air didn't feel bad where I was.

I radioed to Doug, behind me, regarding the sock, watched it for another round, and began the approach. The plane felt good and stable until, just before crossing the river on short final, it was pulled down by the most vicious downdraft I've ever experienced. There was no chance of going around, and flaps were already full.

I immediately summoned all 300 turbocharged horses from the engine, but they weren't quite enough. Working the elevator between stall and fly, up and down, I made it across the river, and barely to the beginning of the strip. Then the downdraft got the better of us and we hit hard enough to fold the nose gear and hit the prop.

The aircraft didn't have shoulder harnesses, but my bleeding nose was the only injury. The passengers continued with their rafting trip, no doubt tickled to be on the water. The aircraft was repaired and flown out, and for several years I thought the file on the story was complete. I had been happy with my reflexes and instincts, getting everything off and the passengers out, and understandably unhappy with just about everything else. And of course, the episode haunted me. What could I have done? Had the damage been avoidable? Why that terrible air with no really fair warning, as there usually is?

Answers came a few years later, in a very interesting book called *The Middle Fork and the Sheepeater War* by Cort Conley and Johnny Carey. It mentioned the Mortar Creek fire, which had only been about five air miles from the Simplot airstrip, in connection with a recorded phenomenon: at just about noon on August 5, 1979, high altitude reconnaissance aircraft registered what they called a secondary ignition of the fire. A sudden fire explosion sent the fire's own cumulonimbus cloud up to 30,000 feet or so. It was too turbulent at that altitude to permit an infrared scan. The films the next day showed that the fire had grown 20,000 acres in one day.

A major fire generates its own weather, and the forces can be virtually identical to those of a thunderstorm. I am now convinced that what I felt during that approach was a microburst, caused by the exploding fire. A case of being at the wrong place at the right time. Doug, after circling long enough for us to move the airplane, experienced no downdraft whatsoever.

Microburst: A fancy new word (in 1979) for a phenomenon that has been around forever. The airlines talk about it a lot these days, as does the FAA. Downdraft, sink, microburst, all basically the same thing, various patterns of upset air, all know to upset aircraft. Every pilot has heard accounts of airplanes being ripped apart during a thunderstorm. I've seen areas in the backcountry where a microburst from a thunderstorm has ripped mature trees out by their roots, sometimes twenty or thirty acres of them.

Sane pilots tend to shy away from thunderstorms. During all phases of flight. The season for thunderstorms is coming. Stay away from them, and anything else that may cause strong, unexpected downdrafts.

Take it from a guy who learned the hard way.

Last month's question was, on your return trip, will you make up the time you lost against a headwind? And how long will each leg be (20 knot wind, 100 knots to cover, 100 knot groundspeed with no wind?)

The answer is no. The time will not be made up, because you have spent more time in the headwind than you will spend in the tailwind. The whiz wheel shows that the 100-knot trip will take 75 minutes in the headwind, and 50 minutes in the tailwind. We lost 15 minutes and made up 10. To break even we'd have to make the 100 knots in 45 minutes. I'll be darned.

Now, as they say, the rest of the story. Five years after this incident, I was able to have the record expunged, so my aviation record now reads "No violations, no accidents, no incidents". Let's hope it stays that way. But the incident probably should have been classified as an accident, as we later discovered some major structural damage had occurred. As the chief pilot flew it down to a better airstrip for more repairs, he discovered that a bent fuselage had stretched the elevator cables and he had very marginal control at the bottom of a tight, twisting canyon.

The Simplot airstrip is now called Lower Loon, and is sometimes called 1100' long, at least for takeoff. I still remember how hard it was to add full power on short final at such a short airstrip, even though a 207 at full power behind the power curve at gross is not going to do a lot of accelerating.

Microbursts continue to make the scene, and there have been some major accidents, even including airliners, that have succumbed to this severe weather event.

Summer 1988, Volume 6, Issue 4
Aircraft Language

It was to be his last flight with the company. He was moving up to a great corporate job flying jets. He was engaged to be married. He had been a Rhodes scholar. Had also been a Navy carrier fighter jock. No dummy. He was a P3 Orion reserves pilot and an Idaho back country air taxi pilot. He had a reputation for flying by the numbers and could get more out of a Cessna 207 than most of us. This time he was working a Cessna 402 freight hauler.

He was a cool professional, even to the end. Communicating with the tower, he first reported the right engine on fire, said he was caging it and returning to the airport. He next reported that he couldn't get the fire out and that he would land short of the runway. His third, final transmission was, "The wing is coming off. I am going down."

That good man was a friend of mine. A few months after his terrible fatal accident another friend, a mechanic who did some contract maintenance for the freight company, filled in a few more details. Just prior to his final flight leg the pilot had stopped by the hangar and had mentioned that the right engine was running hot and rough, with erratic EGT readings. But he had a schedule to keep and a jet to meet in Utah. And he didn't think the problem was important enough to have the mechanic check it out.

The investigation revealed that an exhaust stack was burned out and had been partially covered with duct tape (not by the mechanic I talked to). 1600-degree heat had been blasting directly on the front aluminum wing spar, which eventually caught fire and failed.

I was upset enough to splutter something about "murderously incompetent maintenance". Without disagreeing with me, the mechanic said something unexpected that I've thought about a good many times since then: "Yes, and that airplane was trying to tell him. Too bad he didn't understand."

How do airplanes talk? I once saw a crazy cartoon showing a grammarian supposedly learning "basic duck" and going "quackQUACK quackquack! Quack Quack Quack Quack with a lot of passion. A duck or two were looking at him with somewhat blank expressions, maybe thinking, "Can't he say anything right?" Communicating with airplanes, though, you don't have to speak, all you have to do is listen, and do something about what you hear, when the machine is screaming, "Fix me!"

Do airplanes have souls? If they do, then surely, they have an instinct for self-preservation. If they don't they still seem to possess something like emotions that express themselves in happy sounds when all the components are working together, doing their thing and doing it well. And if they don't even have emotions, by golly they do have character!

We have long attributed names, personalities, and even souls to objects responsible for safely carrying human beings. The objects include sailing ships, trucks and cars, and airplanes. And everyone knows that supposedly identical models perform and communicate differently. Why? Personality. Even if it is undistinguished at first, while its paint is still fresh, the new machine soon begins to change, and get into sync with its owner. If there gets to be a clash of personalities, the owner parts company with the machine. More often, the owner gets very attached and develops a serious relationship with the object.

For us pilots, there is a definite plus to such relationships. You get to know your aircraft, inside and out, better than anyone else. Your ear is so attuned that you know just how your plane is feeling on any given day. You are attentive to its soul, its emotions, and especially its ailments. That understanding is important. Learn your bird's language and it can save both your lives.

If it shows a nasty disposition, a devilish streak, giving you one problem after another, think about dumping it. But first ask yourself, "Have I been treating my machine like a machine? Have I been honestly listening to its complaints? Have I developed a good bedside, or wing side, manner?" Patients resent doctors that treat them like machines, not taking time to ask how they are feeling or, even worse, doctors that ask the right questions but don't listen to the answers.

Once you start listening to your plane, don't turn it into a hypochondriac by exaggerating its symptoms and over reacting at every little burp or noise. But do remember this: airplane engines very rarely quit cold turkey. They are like people. They get sick and they complain fairly early. Most engine failures are the result of something breaking that has been ailing for a while. Not always, but usually. Sometimes, rarely, they do just keel over, dead as a mackerel. Then you have to be ready for surprises. But if you learn your bird's lingo, there are ever so many surprises you can avoid.

Last month I asked about creatures that defy the laws of aerodynamics. The best known, or at least most defiant, are bumblebees, that have an impossibly large body mass in relation to their small wings, and hummingbirds, some species of which migrate more than two thousand miles. Here are some interesting words on hummingbirds: "Although cinematic pictures of birds on the wing revealed a lot of new information about bird flight, those of hummingbirds did not. Instead it took the invention of the stroboscope to unravel the mysteries of how they fly. Motion pictures made from a camera connected to a stroboscope with a flash duration of 1/100,000 of a second finally allowed the bird's unusual method of flying to be studied properly. The little bird actually begins its flight prior to leaving its perch. One hummingbird was observed to lift itself off a twig after three wing strokes which took place in 7/1000 of a second. Also, when the bird starts to fly, it has already almost reached top speed". (Hummingbirds, Tyrrell and Tyrrell).

An issue of the *Air & Space Smithsonian* magazine recently answered the question about flies landing on inverted surfaces. Peter Bowers of Seattle wrote: I would like to inform the curious pilots who wondered about the fly's abilities that the fly does not land on the ceiling through an aerobatic maneuver like a half roll or half loop. He does it by an acrobatic maneuver, a half-somersault. Some British scientists asked the same question a few years ago. They had at their disposal the means to find out. Using strobe lights and high-speed sequence cameras, they found that the fly approaches the ceiling in level flight, raises its forefeet to the ceiling to make contact, then pivots about on those feet to come to rest on the inverted surface." Who knew? Sounds like Spiderman with wings to me.

Fall 1988, Volume 6, Issue 5
Flight Plans and Compasses

This month's column is about telling people where you're heading, and heading where you tell people; or, in both cases, how to avoid taking a turn for the worse.

Over and over again, we've read what appears to be the FAAs favorite accident report liturgy, "The pilot had not filed a flight plan." The implication, all too often, is that the pilot's failure to file a flight plan was the real cause of the accident, and I find that suggestion obnoxious.

So what if the pilot hadn't filed a flight plan? Did that cause a break in the oil line? Sometimes the accident report wording would encourage the naïve public assumption that the pilot's fatal error was not recording his flight with the almighty ATC. Like, he should have known that by not filing a flight plan, he was increasing the chances of crashing. Right.

Look where the average Cub pilot flies. The bush, the backcountry, or around the farm or ranch. In those environments, how much good does an FAA flight plan do? Communication aids are marginal and never available when you would like to use them. Weather delays and route changes are routine, and FAA flight plans are just not feasible or handy in those situations.

All the same, there is an argument for the other side. Statistics show that if you have had an accident, but had previously filed a flight plan, the FAA can find you, on the average, within twelve hours. If you had not filed a plan, the FAA will need approximately fourteen days.

Well now, I hate flight plans, but fourteen days is a

long time to live in a fabric shell and eat jerky or whatever happens to be in that Acme Survival Kit.

In the air taxi business, the FAA approves the use of company flight plans. These work well where I come from. The home offices have radio contact with most of the wilderness ranches, as well as other aircraft in the area. If you are down for weather or a passenger delay, the backcountry grapevine will reliably get the message back to home base. The office has all the information the FAA would have on a flight plan and will notify the officials if necessary. There are times when no immediate contact can be made, usually before actual searching is begun. I don't mind that. It's kind of nice to know someone is doing something about my well-being if I'm going to be gone that long.

But what about the little guy or gal out alone? I suggest developing some kind of flight plan system that will work for you. One pilot I know keeps a slate board on the wall at his ranch, with his aircraft type, N number, and color marked permanently on top. Underneath he writes in the time, where he is going, when he should be back, and who is with him. On the bottom, permanently, are FAA phone numbers and other pertinent numbers and names.

The man has a good idea, worth imitating. It pays to train someone, one way or another, to know how to take care of you, and then regularly provide the updated information that person needs. Nobody gets a bigger pain from flight plans than I do. All the same, every time I fly, someone has the best information I can offer on my vital stats. Unless fourteen days on your own sounds like fun, please give some thought to "anti-isolation insurance."

This morning, as I was coming into Boise after a coyote cruising session, ATC gave me vectors for radar identification. Even though I gave them my exact position, a known reporting point, they made me turn ninety degrees left for ten miles anyway. These guys in the ARSAs want us all to have transponders, it seems. Now the instrument panel on my Cub is typical, including a pretty good magnetic compass. As I cranked around from a northerly to a westerly heading, the crazy thing headed the opposite way, after lagging momentarily. As ATC cleared me back to the north, the compass behavior was not nearly that erratic.

At least there is some consistency to the way a compass temporarily fibs to you. From southerly headings, the compass heads the right way, but it gets in a big hurry, faster than the airplane. From east or west, it acts relatively sane. Unless you speed up or slow down, of course. Speed up and it will try to head north, slow down and it heads south, maybe with a hint of a slow Texas drawl.

This perversity is caused by what the big boys call magnetic dip, the tendency of the compass needles to point down as well as to the magnetic pole. Dip is greatest at the poles and least at the equator. If turns could be made with wings level, the compass would be easier to read. But the mounting of the compass puts its center of gravity below the pivot point on the pedestal. When the wing is lowered or raised, the compass card is banked, and the magnet dips to the low side of the turn, causing the error.

How do you read the little bugger in flight? I rely on "UNOS"; Undershoot north turns because the compass is lagging behind. Overshoot south turns because the compass will indicate a faster turn than the airplane is actually making. The other formula is ANDS when easterly or westerly. Acceleration will show a turn to North, and Deceleration will show a turn to South. Accelerate North, Decelerate South.

What helps more than anything, though, is to watch the compass as you fly and get used to its idiosyncrasies. It comes in handy when ATC wants headings, or when you want to grid an area. For turns to headings, use a shallow bank. Turning towards north, lead the heading (undershoot) an amount equal to the latitude plus half and angle of bank. So at 45 degrees latitude in a 15 degree bank, lead a 90 degree turn by 52 degrees (45 + 15/2). Turning south, overshoot the heading an amount equal to the latitude minus half the angle of bank, or 38 degrees (45-15/2).

Clear as L.A. haze? Practicing in the airplane may be the only way to clear it up.

Well, I have to say I had forgotten about most of this article until reviving it. Funny thing is, I was flying into Boise just the other day in a friend's airplane, and ATC started giving him headings. His GPS page was not up with the heading, and he instinctively began trying to align his directional gyro with his magnetic compass, while trying to turn to the approximate heading, and it was pretty funny to watch! Maybe there is still something to these ancient old practices. (And yet, time does show the age of this article. Today, we have satellite tracking and communication devices which have definitely changed survival tactics in the backcountry.)

Winter 1988, Volume 6, Issue 6
Safety By The Numbers

1. The poor man's carb temp gauge: Your EGT can double as a carb ice detector. Either at normal or low speed cruise, with the EGT set somewhere between 50 and 100 degrees rich, you will notice a cooling on the gauge before the engine slows or runs rough. When you pull the heat on, the gauge shows even more cooling as it richens, and comes back to normal as you take the heat off. In winter flying, when I have to throttle back for long stretches while cruising for coyotes, I'm grateful for the extra instrument, and watch it pretty closely.

2. A good tails-up turn (thanks to Dave Low): Dave is pretty new at this profession, with only about 6000 hours in Cubs, not to mention twice that amount in helicopters, 180s and Cheyennes. When Dave speaks, Cub pilots listen. I overheard him helping a pilot who had been taught, as most of us have, to taxi with the stick back against the stop, to keep the tail down. Dave said that when you put the stick forward, turning on a bad surface, you unweight the tail, put less strain on the tailwheel structure, and turn the airplane more easily. He's right!

3. Get a new picture of stall speed variables (courtesy of Hal Terry of Kodiak, AK): Hal, a long time professional who flies for the Alaska Dept. of Fish and Game, sent a very informative response to a question brought up in this column a few months back. Hal learned about Va

as a Navy cadet about 40 years ago. His graph shows the relationship between airspeed and G forces, and that Va is the speed at which accelerated stall speed crosses the maximum G limit. And he sent us, bolstered by a graph, a detailed, accurate account of what happens to Va with flap and load factor changes. In calibrating the relationship between airspeed and Gs, Hal's graph shows, for example, that if your aircraft is at or below Va and you try to exceed 3.8 Gs, you will stall first. The graph gives details of how extending flaps and/or lightening weight will lower Va.

As a practical application of the data, Hal recommends staying between Va and Vy (96 and 65, respectively, at gross, in a Cub), anytime there's wind and turbulence. According to the amount the Cub's weight falls under 1750 pounds, you fly below the published Va; but to maintain maximum climb capability if you need it, you stay above Vy.

"For some airplanes," Hal says, "you can simply multiply the flaps up stall speed times the square root of the load factor limit and get Va...for the Super Cub, this yields 92 mph; less than the flight manual value of 96. But I use it because it's on the conservative side. Also, the flight manual uses the old fashioned 'true indicated airspeed' which equates to 'calibrated airspeed'. But you look at indicated airspeed in the cockpit. Another reason to be conservative."

Speaking for myself, thanks Hal! Information like this from a veteran who knows his stuff can reduce flying risks for a lot of us.

4. In winter, keep your ice peeled; and keep the fog off the windshield, too, because loss of vision during takeoff can be as hazardous as ice on the wings. This little plug on safety features the defroster sold by Jim's Cub Crafters. If, some wet and snowy morning, looking out your windshield was like trying to see out of a latrine window, you understood what an important safety device a good defroster is. Jim's works well; it is a dependable friend.

5. Keep the mice away from your plane if you don't want damage to the rib stitching or other vital parts that look delicious and homey to Mickey and his friends. If you keep your Cub in a mousy hangar, the critters will see welcome signs pinned to each wheel unless you take some pains to discourage them. The inhospitable treatment we give them is to sprinkle mothballs around the tires. Smells bad, looks funny, but tells the varmints to get lost.

6. Taxing in a crosswind: The Cub is so light that control positions in a crosswind are critical. Sometimes it's not enough. You can land into the wind, but it is just blowing too hard to safely turn crosswind without some help from wingtip walkers. With a radio and people to listen to it (or today, cellphones), you can idle into the wind until help comes. Without help, it's a good idea to be able to pull straight into a tie down into the wind after landing, have your passenger help while staying out of the prop, or having some other plan before landing.

But if the wind allows crosswind and downwind taxing, it's important to have the controls in the proper position. Into the wind, neutral aileron and neutral to aft elevator. Right quartering headwind, right aileron and aft elevator. Right crosswind, right aileron and neutral elevator. Tailwind, neutral aileron and forward elevator. Left quartering tailwind, right aileron and forward elevator. Left cross or left quartering headwind, left aileron and neutral to aft elevator.

It's a little confusing until you practice, kind of like patting your head and rubbing your belly. During crosswind practice I have students do 360s on the run-up pad, moving the controls all the way around. Think of the aileron being into the wind when the wind is in front of the wing, and the aileron being away from the wind when the wind is behind the wing. Forward elevator keeps the tail down in a tailwind, and opposite aileron keeps the wing down in a quartering tailwind. The quartering tailwind is the most vulnerable position for a tailwheel airplane. It calls for slow speed and extreme caution. And for practice until it come automatically. The old FAA adage "turn into dive away" is helpful to some.

Spring 1989, Volume 7, Issue 1
Accident Probabilities

Even in a nice dependable Super Cub, there can be moments that test your poise. Suppose, for instance, you are on your way back from a nice airing. You have picked up just enough small signals to make you decide that maintenance has been a bit marginal, and you had better do something about it. Then, suddenly, you have a problem: at the welding on the cable tab, the cable to your right rudder pedal breaks. How do you keep your peace of mind, to say nothing of your neck?

When that happened to me, the next few minutes were not exactly peaceful, but at least they didn't cost me my neck. Approaching the airport with power off, I kept my left hand on the stick, and my right hand on the rear right rudder pedal. This made for the kind of landing I hadn't practiced for, and if I had had a gorilla's long right arm the touchdown might have been smoother. But that was one time I believed the old saying, "If you walked away, it was a good landing."

As a survivor of that episode, I have made rudder pedals a fairly regular preflight item. Funny how long, and vividly, you remember certain things. And with a Cub, a preflight can be as thorough as you want. No airplane I know of has more exposed parts and pieces.

Quite a while ago, Jim sent me some NTSB PA-18 accident reports from 1981 and 1982. The other day, thinking about the broken rudder incident as having had the potential for a serious accident, I decided to get some perspective on the factors behind plane crashes. The stats were interesting and informative. Out of 95 investigated accidents for the two-year period, 23 involved stalls, 24 were ground loops, 22 were power plant/ fuel problems, four were landing gear failures, seven were the result of buzz jobs, and the remaining 15 came from an assortment of causes as varied as locked controls, bad weather, and alcohol.

That information led me to the special study AOPA did in July, 1986, of fifty Cub accidents that had happened between 1983 and 1986. Of those, 20% were fuel related (three serious), 16% were taxi/ground loop problems, 12% were stall/spin (all serious), 6% were low flying maneuvers (all serious), and 25% were "overconfidence accidents".

The number of accidents was a surprise. Forty-seven a year for one particular model of aircraft is not peanuts. That is almost one in every state per year, although most reports were from Alaska and the western U.S. There is a rumor that insurance companies don't like Cubs, and the records suggest why that may be so.

The stats also show that stall, ground loop, and power plant problems are all about equal, and collectively account for about three-fourths of the accidents. Of the three groups, ground loop accidents are the least serious. Most could have been avoided with adequate training and equipment. Though they are embarrassing and damaging, these accidents are rarely deadly.

The power plant failures were surprisingly frequent. Many of them were fuel related, a mostly inexcusable factor. Maybe Cubs tend to have more home maintenance than other planes do.

The small percentage of weather related accidents was encouraging. It appears that most Cub pilots are savvy enough to understand that they aren't flying weather proof machines. Most of us, having once tried to outrun a thunderstorm, or having survived an attempt at IFR on needle, ball, and unheated airspeed, have decided that such games are too much like Russian roulette.

One report, though, follows the trail of a pilot who failed to learn from experience, and as you read you may be smiling in spite of yourself:

> On 2/16/82, the county sheriff received information that the pilot had wrecked his aircraft on 2/13/82. He went to the scene and observed the aircraft in an inverted position on snow covered terrain. On 2/20/82, he received information that the pilot had another accident. The sheriff went out again and found the aircraft on its top about 2 or 3 miles southwest of the location of the first mishap. He also noted that the pilot's tractors and one pick up truck were located where a runway had been plowed at the location of the first mishap. A doctor that examined the pilot after the crash stated that the pilot said he had been hunting coyotes. The pilot was uncooperative in providing information concerning the accident. According to FAA records, the pilot had no valid pilot license or medical certificate. His previous license had been revoked. Final Score: Coyotes 2 // Super Cub 0

The third large grouping, stall accidents, is one you

can't shrug off. Those accidents nearly always cause injury or death. And they are avoidable. These Cubs we like so much will fly very slowly, turn very sharply. But go too slow, or turn too sharp, and they quit flying, just like any other airplane.

Most pilots fly their airplanes conservatively for the first forty or fifty hours. Then they get a little cocky. The one-hundred-hour mark is statistically a dangerous time. So is 500. And 1000. And 5000. The moral is, watch out for "record numbers" that tempt you to get too sure of yourself. We continue to go through periods of over confidence throughout our entire careers, regardless of time and experience. It helps to be aware of the susceptibility. When we're feeling cocky and ready to fly the airplane slower and steeper, it's time to get some dual, or at least go up to altitude and re-familiarize ourselves with full power, full flap banked stalls, cross control stalls, and so forth. We've got to know exactly where and how our aircraft will stall, especially if we're going to fly it close to that speed.

Last month's question was, "What turns the airplane in flight?" This is a classic FAA flight instructor oral exam question. The answer your examiner is not looking for is the rudder. Rudders turn boats, not airplanes. The ailerons turn (bank) the airplane, and the rudder is there to counteract adverse aileron yaw and help you make a nice coordinated turn.

One FAA inspector I know likes to argue, facetiously, that the elevator turns the aircraft, and he uses a Lear jet in a roll as an example. Another answer, perhaps the best, is that turn is the resultant factor of inputs from all three controls.

Today, we have some excellent resources to refer to. Take, for example, this video from Rich Stowell: *http://youtu.be/nWbk3jn0GK4*

Summer 1989, Volume 7, Issue 2
Two Versus Three, Slip Versus Crab

You've turned base to final and discovered a 90-degree gusty crosswind for landing. Your fuel gauge insists that you go ahead and land anyway, and your head adds a cautionary note: "Please, not just 'anyway'; it had better be the right way, the way that will keep my Cub in one piece." So, instantly reviewing safety options, you remember two approved possible ways to approach the strip, and two more good touchdown techniques. Which do you choose?

First decision: In compensating for the crosswind on your approach, do you dip the upwind wing down to control drift, using whatever rudder is necessary to keep the nose-to-tail line the same as the runways? Or do you crab into the wind, cocking the airplane the necessary degrees into the wind to prevent drift?

Second decision: When it's time to touchdown, will you do it on the upwind main first, then the downwind main, followed by the tailwheel (the classic crosswind wheel landing), or kick the airplane straight and touch the upwind main and tailwheel together, followed closely by the downwind main (the three-point "stall" landing)?

The ideal moment for weighting your alternatives would not appear to be while you are bouncing around a few hundred feet above a landing strip in moderate turbulence, but preferable might be a time like now, when you are taking comfort from a cup of coffee, maybe, and reviewing the advice of your friendly safety columnist. And what your friendly safety columnist recommends is that you practice all four techniques so thoroughly that in a real situation after a quick assessment of the variable conditions that go along with your crosswind problem, you will proceed smoothly and confidently to cope, and the right techniques will come naturally.

A few years ago, I wouldn't have given this advice on approaches, because I so firmly preferred the "slip" to the "crab." A slip keeps you in tune with the airplane, easily feeling gusts and changes in wind force and direction, compensating for them and preparing for what you will find close to the ground.

You don't have to worry about the exact moment to switch from crab to landing attitude. Recently, though, I have had to recognize the value of the crab when passenger comfort is a heavy factor. In a substantial aircraft like the Twin Otter, throwing nineteen passengers over to one side of the cabin during a long, altitude-restricted final approach is just not cool. And even in a Super Cub, when you have only one or two passengers, they are probably friends, and you might want to be nice to them.

The factors in "wheel" versus "stall" landings are just as clear cut as those in approaches, but harder to evaluate. If you follow the "wheels" sequence—upwind main, downwind main, tailwheel—you have advantages in visibility, aileron control, and power curve and speed. (But speed is also a serious disadvantage in a short field landing; it increases the likelihood of bouncing; and some short strips just don't allow that waste of distance). A wheel landing may enhance your ability to pick the best moment, between gusts, perhaps, to be most vulnerable, just before all three wheels bear weight.

In some circumstances, though, the stall landing—slow, behind the power curve—is hard to beat. When the bird touches down, she is done flying, and that "final touch" gives you a good feeling when you're staring at the bushy end of a short strip. If there is a bounce, it generally won't be a problem unless you have failed to control vertical and horizontal speed.

A friend of mine, with years of flying taildraggers from Cubs to 185s to Corsairs, will not do a wheel landing, regardless of the conditions. I don't think he's ever ground looped, and I'm not about to hint even a word of advice to him.

But I know some other short field masters who could give him a hard time. Their preference is for a special kind of wheel landing, the tail low variety. They approach in a three-point attitude, then roll the tail up slightly to touch on the mains. They have the three-point advantage of a slow approach, plus the wheel advantage of control and visibility. The drawback is that those landings require skill and constant practice, especially in my case, when I'm flying a 185 at the aft cg limit.

One point of agreement among veterans is this: no one seems to like tail high wheel landings. The airplane looks vulnerable and fast, with the rudder that high. And even though everyone has a preference, which sometimes has the status of "the only way to do it", I maintain that there is and ought to be more than one way to shoot an approach, skin a coyote, or grease a landing. Though slip approaches are perhaps becoming a lost art, all my students get exposed to it. And they don't solo until they can do both wheel and stall landings.

This completes my argument that every tailwheel pilot should be familiar with both types of approaches and landings, as comfortable with one type as another (today, this is in the regulations). You are then resourceful enough to be able to decide which is better for which conditions. Extra skills can provide an extra margin of safety.

One word of caution for new wheel-landers: if you begin bouncing on contact, do not try to salvage a landing after more than two bounces. The oscillations quickly compound themselves, developing into a very dangerous porpoising that will cause a loss of control. The only remedy is to add power, level off, and try again. And as with anything new with an airplane, don't try short field stuff until you are proficient.

To Paul Drennon, of Helena: Yes, I have been on the airstrip you mentioned, in my own Super Cub, many times. Your question brought up several points regarding special equipment for rough field operations.

We are all aware that the Cub's weak point is its landing gear. The stock set up is just not strong enough for constant abuse on rough fields. On my airplane, I started at the tail end, with a PA-25 Pawnee tail spring. Then I put on the 8" Scott tailwheel assembly with the two-hole attachment. A Cub-operating crop duster recommended that set up to me after he had broken a couple of the one-hole Scotts. Neither he nor I have had any trouble with that arrangement.

On the main gear, I replaced the aluminum bungee covers with the vinyl J-3 covers, for ease of inspection, went to 8:50 x 6 tires with the Cleveland double-puck brakes, and the Super Master Cylinder STC. We also installed gear safety cables. Because I couldn't afford the heavy-duty Alaska Gear Vees, we elected to go with the older style gear beef mod, which consists of inserting a length of 4130 into the hollow axle. This strengthens the gear appreciably.

Other niceties for rough ground include the metal belly, leading edge tape for the elevator, and a 20-mph airspeed indicator. I just love going into those short, rough places where the trout grow fat and the elk are safe from 99% of the less fortunate hunters. See you back there!

Speaking from the present, oversize tires have become another great asset and safety addition to backcountry flying. You can read about some of the advantages in "Mountain, Canyon, and Backcountry Flying" (Hoover and Williams, 2019).

Well, today we live in an entirely new world. With the loss of FSSs and the addition of internet, pilots are now learning how to do self-briefings, and we even have the option of live weather in the cockpit. And the weather itself has even changed with climate change. With all that, it is amazing how timely those words from decades ago still are.

Fall 1989, Volume 7, Issue 3
Weather Flying

First, a warning! Mothballs around the tires don't work against mice! Next time, I'll wait until after the annual to pass on words of wisdom regarding Cub upkeep. In years past, we have kept bags of mothballs in the wings and fuselage, and in closed-in spaces like that they do seem to repel the little buggers. But out in the open spaces of a hangar, evidence proves that they do not. During our recent annual we found mouse nests in both the wings and fuselage. Luckily no damage had been done. So, go back to boxes over the tires for the best outside protection I know. We still use mothballs inside the bird, however.

Especially during this time of year, it seems, pressure changes of three to five hundred feet in one hundred miles are not unusual. If you travel to places that don't offer current altimeter settings, or if the Kollsman window in your altimeter isn't all that accurate anyway, it pays to know what to expect in altimeter errors.

It took me forever to figure out a wag to remember what pressure changes did what to the altimeter. I would be sure I had it, and then another one of the FAA's 14 written exams would throw the question at me a different way and confuse me again. Even the saying, "High to low, look out below" didn't completely solve it for me. I had to watch the altimeter during actual flights to decide for myself that if I were flying into a lower pressure area, the altimeter would read higher than I actually was. It does this at a rate of one hundred feet for every tenth of an inch of pressure change (i.e. 30.10 to 30.00). This really isn't critical in VFR flying, until you enter the landing phase. Then it can throw your pattern work off a little.

One exercise to help prevent that is to develop depth perception by not relying on the altimeter. We need to do this in sailplane flying a lot, because we were never entirely sure where we might end up landing. It was important to know what 800 or 1000' AGL looked like. It's easy to practice. When you get to pattern altitude, take a look around. Study what things look like from up there. Same with 1500' and 500'. Then test yourself. It doesn't take long to learn. I routinely fail the cockpit lights on night checkouts, and the student is usually surprised at how close his airspeed and altitude come out when he doesn't have needles to chase. Some of them might even admit it's fun, after the sweat dries.

Pressure changes are one of the minor inconveniences of VFR weather flying, and one easily dealt with as long as the altimeter isn't treated as a critical gauge. The big trick to VFR weather flying is to stay out of IMC weather!

Once IMC weather is encountered, it's a whole new ball game. And a much tougher one. The best instrument pilot I can think of would be in a world of hurt in my

Cub IFR, with basic instruments, basic radio, and not even a heated pitot tube. I've been there—needle, ball, mag compass, and airspeed icing up-and I don't even like to think about it. It's suicidal. Period. Don't, Don't, Don't fly VFR airplanes in IFR weather. End of lecture.

OK, so what about marginal VFR weather? Another story. Just the other day Flight Service told me, "VFR not recommended," and I could see eight-tenths blue sky and 30 miles. Granted, there was a storm coming in, but I had ample time to beat it, and my flight was excellent, VFR all the way. I even had that most-blessed of all events in a Cub—tailwind! However, the day before, prior to starting a day of coyote hunting, flight service had told me it would be "good VFR" all day, and I ended up trying to return to Boise in 500' ceilings, partially obscured, three-quarters of a mile visibility. Not quite good enough for even a special VFR clearance, and I spent the night with friends a hundred miles east.

With that kind of weather, not to mention weather forecasting, how can the pilot of a ninety mile an hour airplane avoid IFR, or even marginal VFR weather? It isn't easy. It takes some understanding of weather patterns, some sixth sense savvy, some intuition, and some forecasting of your own.

I usually don't have any problem with marginal VFR flight in a Cub, as long as the weather is relatively stable and not deteriorating. One of the reasons is the number of landing options in a Cub. Trying to get into Boise the other day, the Flight Service gal audibly relaxed after I told her I was in no trouble and could land on several little dirt tracks in the desert below me if necessary. Another reason is the aircraft's slow speed. However, that low speed is an obvious liability when trying to outrun something, and the aircraft itself is a liability if the marginal VFR stuff turns into IFR. For the local flights, of course, the problem of staying VFR is usually small, except for locales prone to coastal fog or other special weather factors. You look outside, call the experts, ask the locals, make a decision based on all that plus your own experience, and probably have a nice scenic outing.

It is more complicated for the pilot trying to go somewhere. He may not be familiar with local weather or geography. If he isn't his weather minimum will probably increase. If he is, he will have to evaluate what he sees with what he knows. (i.e., it's pretty good right here, but it always gets worse down the canyon about forty miles).

Don't blindly believe what the forecasters say. They are human, some are better than others, and some are luckier than others. That "weather is a science" axiom goes only so far with me. Local pilots can often predict the weather better than the experts. Don't be afraid to ask those locals.

On the other hand, don't boycott the experts. I look at their maps and forecasts all I can. After several years in one state, putting all that together with what actually happens, I occasionally differ with the experts' forecast, and turn out to be right! I know, a 7-year-old could probably do the same thing just guessing.

So, after talking to everyone we can, and feeling good with our own intuition about it, we decide to go. Now comes the real trick, to stay VFR, or alive, which are the same thing. If the weather is forecast to get worse along the route, is it actually doing it, or is it getting worse than forecast? Watch out! Is it windier than forecast, or from a different direction than it should be? Watch that too. Is the weather supposed to be getting better than it is? Safe flight in marginal conditions requires constant vigilance, constant reevaluation of the weather as it is happening. Don't believe in yourself or your weatherman to the extent that you can't believe the weather you are actually experiencing! Un-forecast weather may be more common on the coasts and in the mountains than the flatland, but it happens everywhere, all the time.

So, your forecast weather becomes "un-forecast." The flight was set up with plenty of daylight and shorter legs for fuel, so there's no immediate problem there. The first option, the pilot's best friend, the 180 turn, is initiated as IMC weather looms ahead. Uh-oh. The storm has blown in behind us, blocking the way. Our second option was a nifty little airstrip that sits right where the storm is coming from, so that is out of the question. But we have a third way out, and this time it's a hundred miles out of the way, but it's downwind, and the storm shouldn't be there yet. We've got the fuel, with reserves even, and daylight even though the storm is going to bring darkness a half hour early. Son of a gun, the third option isn't going to work either. That damn storm seems to be settling down from all directions. We're stuck. IFR is not an option. Our fourth option, however, is going to work. There's a great looking little road down there. Stay cool, look it over for obstacles, high and low, wind direction, traffic, a farmhouse nearby, a place to pull off. Relax, concentrate on the short and rough field work we have practiced and know we can do, and get safely on the ground.

We'll tie down, walk to the farmhouse, make a phone call or two, and hope we can trade a couple of airplane rides for a bed and maybe even a hot brandy! Things could be a lot worse. As the old saying goes, I'd a lot rather be down here wishing I was up there, than be up there wishing I was down here.

Have plenty of options at your disposal when working the weather, and don't be bashful about using them.

Winter 1989, Volume 7, Issue 4
On Weathering Weather

Will Rogers was the sage I believe, who expressed the next to last word about weather: "Everybody is always talking about the weather, but no one will ever do anything about it." For pilots, the thought goes one step farther. "If you are always studying the weather, maybe you'll get lucky, and the weather won't do anything about you."

Weather forces are powerful, often mysterious, and generally irresistible, as was pointed out in the last issue. You never know enough about them, but if you don't find out all you can, you are just asking for very serious trouble.

The VFR pilot has to be constantly on the lookout for conditions that threaten VFR flight. On the coasts and in the hills, those conditions can change rapidly, too rapidly to do anything about if you haven't picked up on them soon enough.

Knowing how to gauge lowering ceilings is an important trick to know. Sometimes it's tough to pick up a horizon on hills or water. Experienced weather flyers are constantly watching for even the hint of a lowering ceiling, and the speed at which it is lowering. I have seen them drop close to 2000 fpm in the mountains.

Wind is another factor to watch. It is usually steadier on the flat land, and changes in velocity and/or direction are good indications of a weather change, either for the better or the worse. Knowing the location of storm centers and the rotation of air around them (lows turn counterclockwise in the northern hemisphere) can help determine what is going on. Wind shifts indicate shears or frontal passages.

Flying canyons in weather limits options. You can either pull a 180 or land if there is a place to. A third option, usually not feasible in fog conditions, but more usable in squall conditions, is to calmly circle over a point until the squall passes or move down the canyon in the clear spot between squalls until they move out of the way. To stay calm in those conditions is the hardest part, but lack of fuel or daylight makes it almost impossible to keep from getting panicky. No doubt about it, you're in a tough spot when you are in those conditions.

One of the most dangerous of VFR weather conditions is layered or sandwich fog. It tends to worsen late in the day. If there is a low layer over the water and a higher layer near the canyon rim, it is easy for you to become the center entrée in a nasty, unescapable sandwich, as you become trapped between the two fog layers coming closer and closer together to form a solid layer.

The canyons of Idaho can be especially treacherous. Sandwich fog usually arrives between storms or after frontal passage, when there is still plenty of moisture in the air. As that wet air is trapped over the canyon river water and condenses, it forms water dogs, patches of fog, that can easily expand and develop into solid layers. It isn't unusual to see more than one layer of this fog in the deeper canyons. When the ceiling is low and your flight takes you down into those canons, a watchful eye out for sandwich fog could make a difference in whether or not you reach your destination.

I have talked to pilots who became trapped just like that and elected to go IFR to climb out of the canyon.

They were lucky to be able to talk about it. Most of them understood their good fortune very well and look back on their "sandwich" experience as an unforgettable and terrifying moment. I almost became trapped that way myself one late fall day in the backcountry. That's how I know the condition is fear inspiring. The experience taught me three things, especially, that I won't forget:
1. Realize that darkness falls much earlier with fog and overcast.
2. Watch behind to keep an escape route.
3. Never mess with layered fog unless you are intimately familiar with the geography and the possible landing sites.

Another trick in weather flying is not to be afraid to use the radio. Cub pilots have a built-in aversion to radios. I leave mine off a lot of the time. It takes too much of the enjoyment out of the flight. Cub flying is back to basics flying, to be done with the door open whenever possible. But radios can be a useful tool and helpful with weather problems, provided you haven't waited until the weather has already pushed you too low for reception. Flight Service Stations provide another source for current weather, forecasts, and even an occasional phone call to uncontrolled fields for current weather information. The other day, one friendly FSS employee volunteered to make three phone calls to uncontrolled fields for me, trying to find a VFR field.

It took me years to become even mildly interested in weather theory. The FAA exams do nothing to encourage interest in it. But I have learned that an understanding of the science of weather, plus the art of interpreting data, can go a long way in predicting flying conditions.

Learning about weather, even VFR type, is a huge subject that is impossible to completely cover in a couple of editorials. Like the rest of aviation, it is a never-ending process. I recommend studying and analyzing storm patterns in the country you fly, and how they affect flying conditions, and being sure that you do it from the ground when conditions are unsafe for flight.

In this and the last issue on VFR weather, I have emphasized at least five points:

1. Although we all make fun of Flight Service occasionally for their crazy predictions and "VFR flight not recommended" attitudes when it is obviously okay, their data is important. So is their interpretation of it. But so is yours.
2. By studying weather patterns in your area, and by increasing your understanding of weather theory, your interpretation of data will complement the information you get from the pros.
3. Keep a watchful eye while airborne, to see what is happening with the weather and to try to analyze and understand it, and to store it away for future reference.
4. Leave yourself extra options while flying in weather.
5. Most importantly, don't let yourself get into IMC conditions. Once in them, you've lost all options.
6. Listen to your intuition, your sixth sense, about weather, and how you feel about it.

Spring 1990, Volume 8, Issue 1
Attitude Adjustment

Do you seek a few contrasts, even from your favorite line of work? Some peace and quiet after hours of radio static and engine noise, coolness after the heat, relaxation after sustained concentration? An ice-cold beer after a long hot day of flying; that's my idea of the perfect attitude adjustment.

But if you aren't willing or able to ground yourself for the next eight hours, there are other ways to adjust. Some of those ways are so good, in fact, that I come pretty close to recommending them as an alternative to liquid refreshment (I am not crazy enough to come any closer to that recommendation than "pretty close").

The attitude with which we approach and perform our "art" is crucial. (Whether it's work or pleasure, hard or easy, challenge or diversion, I hope flying is always, through it all, considered an art). The old jet jock may consider flying just a job. The young instructor or charter pilot may have something to prove. The inexperienced private pilot may think he's got it mastered and there's nothing to it. The difference is, an artist always tries to do better.

The qualified pilots in the world bring a whole multitude of attitudes and combinations of attitudes into their cockpits. Some are safer than others. The Canadian Civil Aviation Authority has labeled five "bad flying attitudes" as particularly unsafe. All five are emotional patterns; and each pattern is one in which thinking has either been postponed or jettisoned altogether.

The Hip Shooter is the guy or gal who isn't willing to finish evaluating a situation before acting on it. If the situation happens to turn bad, and the pilot survives at all, there may be some moments for theoretical good judgment as the aircraft lies on its back in a snowdrift, or as the pilot rests in the comfort and solitude of a hospital bed. I came close to becoming a good illustration some years ago, on a hunting trip. My inducements to a hip shooting decision were three huge bull elk watching me from a ridge. The temptation was to land my stock Cub on a steep hillside at 8500'. After about fifteen approaches, each ending with me peeling off to the canyon, some thought processes returned in spite of all my heroic efforts to resist them. They informed me that such impulsive behavior was appalling; an attempted landing among those rocks would damage the plane and add a new case to a history of hazards of "bull fever."

The Immortalist, in the spirt of superman, hardly needs an airplane to fly. Sweet comfort probably emerges from that attitude, as long as it works, and when it ceases to work the Immortalist may never know what happened—or anything else. Basically, what the Immortalist has practiced is substituting an emotional condition of pride or faith for plain, ordinary reasonableness. "Nothing bad can happen to me, because I'm nice." An experienced immortalist pilot of my acquaintance actually does happen to be a man of the cloth, and for all I know God *is* his co-pilot. He's run out of gas at least once, and once made a Christmas Eve approach to a VFR only field, in a mountain valley, during a blizzard. Maybe he was following a star in the East nobody else could see. The town still talks about it, but many of its residents won't fly with the man.

In this column I have no intention of interfering with the subject of theology, but at an early age I was encouraged to believe that heaven may be inclined to help those who help themselves. Taking the opposite view in an airplane may be a little like flying with your eyes shut and your thinking machinery turned off.

The Macho Man, and whatever is the female equivalent, doesn't always have a hairy chest, just a hairy brain. The problem may be thinking too much, not really thinking, but indulging an emotional determination not to lose face, or act in any way that hints of flabby muscles or weak nerves. You can get so afraid of looking indecisive or timid that you block out the outside situation itself, or pretend it is something different than it really is. A surviving Macho pilot usually has pretty good hands, quick reactions, and an attitude that paralyzes thought processes just when they are needed. One man I know who fits this mold is exceptionally skillful, and thanks to his macho attitude he has wrecked no fewer than six airplanes.

The Quitter has the reputation of being a person who thinks too much, and just isn't gutsy enough to hang on and keep trying even when there seems to be no hope. Another interpretation is that the quitter takes some probable outcome to be a fact, and thereupon abandons all further thought. When braver people are jumping to safety, the quitter jumps to conclusions. You want the advice of a smart, brave man? Well, nobody ever accused Yogi Berra of being an intellectual, but one of his often-quoted remarks goes right up there beside the best: "It (the old ball game) it ain't over till it's over."

Students and inexperienced pilots sometimes lack the confidence, and curiosity, to keep flying their craft until it stops, no matter what. They become passengers along for the ride, victims of fate. And when things get dicey, even experienced pilots must fight eruptions of panic that block rational thought. But some pilots have become legendary because they never quit trying, and thinking, during a crisis. Even with wings threatening to fall off! An English poet invented kind of a neat phrase for that capacity to function under pressure, completely uncertain of outcomes. The phrase was "negative capability" (John Keats). It says to me that courage is partly the ability to overcome obstacles to thinking.

The Rebel doesn't like to be told what to do by people or agencies that haven't proved worthy of respect. This anti-authority figure takes a short cut from thinking by reverting to an evaluation of the source rather than taking a fresh look at the actual information or orders from that source. How I know this is, I'm talking about myself. I'm also sadly talking about a man I saw taking off in a state of anger and frustration toward an authority figure (me). We'll never know just what led up to the accident that killed and burned his passenger and him, but I'll go on believing that if he had been able to think as well on the flight as he usually did, he would be alive today.

Not sure where you are, but afraid to ask, and look bad? **Macho pilot,** unclear on the concept "knowledge is power." Conditions are bad, going to take off anyway? The **invulnerable pilot,** committed to flying with mental eyes shut. Muttering to yourself, "I know the idiot who claims my plane wasn't made for that airstrip, and whatever he says, I'll believe the opposite?" **Anti-authority figure,** neglecting to separate the source and the truth. If the engine quits, so do you? **Resignation figure,** inclined to give up thinking, because it's too hard. Find yourself about to land at that little airstrip, because there's a creek nearby that promises good fishing? **Impulsive pilot,** willing to postpone thinking until it's too late.

So, we've spent some time on poor and dangerous attitudes. What's a good attitude? The pilots I respect have a laid back, relaxed style with a suspicious streak and the ability to say no. They are suspicious because they have had enough surprises that they will gather all the information they can from other pilots, windsocks, Unicoms, and what have you, compile all that with their own observations, and then never be complacent enough to completely believe what they hear, or that it will stay that way. And they have nothing to prove. It often appears that the pilots with the best attitudes are the ones with the biggest yellow stripes down their backs.

The attitude that enables a pilot to say no, to loads, weather, or destinations, is even more critical. This is usually not an inborne trait. Especially with the beginning charter pilot, typically out to please his boss and prove himself, not feeling comfortable about saying no makes for a dangerous situation. Learning to say no is one of the most important lessons a pilot can learn. It is the same attitude that makes the 180 degree turn easy to do.

Emotions have no place in the cockpit. They cannot be allowed to affect a pilot's attitude. A 17th century philosopher by the name of Baruch Du Spinoza said that "emotions are incomplete ideas." With that thought in mind, trade your emotions for the real thing while in the cockpit.

Well-known editorialist Paul Bertorelli recently commented on the five hazardous attitudes in a humorous but thoughtful way: He reports that in a conversation with the legendary instructor John King, John commented, "Hell, you have to have three of those just to want to be a pilot in the first place." Then Bertorelli wrote, "My three are that I have resigned myself to my antiauthoritarian impulsivity and so far my machismo has rendered me untouchable. I guess I'm over budget."

My father was a big help on this one, with his obvious ending.

Summer 1990, Volume 8, Issue 2
Judgment Day

Last month the subject was mostly "attitudes that don't help you survive." This month the subject is "judgment that does help keep you alive." Actually, both months we're talking pilot quality, including ways of turning a "pretty good pilot" into a class act. I define class act as a pilot with outstanding skills, knowledge, and judgment.

People tend to assume that experience and judgment have a fixed direct ratio to each other—the greater a pilot's experience, the better that pilot's judgment. FAA accident files, unfortunately, warn that such an assumption isn't true. So, to cultivate good judgment, we'd better begin by seeing it as separable from experience. The pilot who fails to use experience is one who lacks good judgment; the pilot with really bad judgment is one who deliberately ignores the lessons of experience.

I believe good judgment to be a decision-affecting factor that never gives up or goes away. In the quality pilots I've observed, judgment is not an occasional thing; it operates before, during, and after a flight, like breathing; applying experience to situations at hand, continually sorting things out. Every day is judgment day, and every minute is judgment minute.

What a pilot judges is "the odds." That requires

seeing situations clearly, understanding one's personal limitation, recognizing new and unknown factors, quickly selecting experience and knowledge that could apply, and making honest calculations.

For example, take the figuring you do on daylight, weather, and fuel. With lots of fuel and daylight, you might choose to fight some weather. But if you are also running low on daylight, your options, and odds, have sharply dropped. If you are low on both daylight and fuel, facing bad weather, you have virtually no options, and Nick the Greek would be inclined to bet against you. There are other factors affecting the odds: how well you know the territory and how well trained you are for it, for example. But, "the superior pilot uses his superior judgment to avoid having to use his superior skills." That's an old and very truthful saying.

After listening to my betters in the aviation world for quite a few years, I am now prepared to share some of their tips on improving one's judgment.

1. The raw material of judgment is experience, which unfortunately takes time to accumulate. Survival, in the meanwhile, requires conservatism, luck, and caution. At the start of your flying career, those provide almost your only margin of safety.

2. One role of judgment is to set your limits and safety standards. Those limits can expand as you are able to add experience and skill; and the limits can become more flexible as you are able to evaluate conditions of the airfield, the plane, and the weather. The more you

know, however, the more likely you are to see that you have been overestimating your odds, and you may well decide not to expand your limits but reduce them.

3. A malady that has probably affected every pilot at one time or another is get-home-itis. Be prepared to recognize and fight its symptoms.

4. Learn to think backwards from consequences to causes and beginnings. Is it wise to invest one million hours (or the rest of your life) in one dangerous, possibly disastrous flying hour? Thinking about what follows from poor judgment can go a long way in creating good judgment, because it heightens one's understanding of what is at risk. Life.

5. Face the realization that it is okay to break the airplane, bruise the ego, or get caught in an FAA violation, if the alternative is injury of death. Too many statistics are former pilots who were too embarrassed to turn around, or too afraid to risk damaging an airplane. Make up your mind now that when necessary you will take lifesaving action, regardless of other consequences. It's the ultimate policy in minimizing losses.

6. Observe the legends in the field, to learn what you can by their example; and study the decisions of a first-rate flight instructor. If your teacher happened to abort a flight-a decision that may have saved your life-find out the reasoning. What did the pilot judge the odds to be, as affected by, say, bad visibility, an airplane condition, or a late weather report?

7. Read accident reports. Not because you're morbid, but because you prefer to learn new ways to stay alive.

8. The toughest judgment to acquire is intuitive, the ability to make use of subliminal cues such as weather trends, how you and your aircraft feel. But though time and experience will sharpen that intuitive judgment, year by year, you can practice one good principle from now on: listen for warnings. Take them more seriously than positive impulses. If what you're about to do doesn't feel right, don't do it!

9. Learn all you can about your own decision-making processes and the ways they are distorted and weakened by stress.

So, for now, I respectfully suggest that a good way to develop strong judgment is to exercise it.

> "Weary with Toil, I haste me to my bed,
> The dear repose for limbs with travel tired;
> But then begins a journey in my head
> To work my mind, when body's work's expired…"

Shakespeare, Sonnet 27

Fall 1990, Volume 8, Issue 3
Decision Making and Stress

Sherry Knight-Rossiter, formerly of Progressive Pilot Seminars, pus on excellent weekend ground schools and refresher clinics. I gathered the following section of material from one of her past CFI clinics:

Decision-making is taking the action; passing judgment on the issue under consideration. That requires thinking, which can be broken down into five levels: the top level is **Critical Thought,** which is objectively and open-mindedly examining the options and bare facts. The second level is **Rational Thought,** which will include a person's preconceived myths and biases. **Reactive Thought,** the third level, is automatic reaction to input, doing the first thing that comes to mind. The fourth level is **Irrational Thought,** doing the wrong thing, and the bottom level is **Panic,** where no action takes place.

Relate this to the Poor Judgment Chain, where a series of poor judgments and decisions leads to an accident. This breaks down into three levels: First, the pilot either does or doesn't do. If he does, he may either over do or under do. Finally, he may do too early, or he may do too late.

For example, a pilot doesn't turn around when it would have been a good decision, good judgment, to have done so. Or, he overdoes it and makes an emergency landing when a simple 180-degree turn would have sufficed. Or, he takes action too late, and slams into the hill in the middle of the turn, IMC. So simply taking action is not enough. A pilot must decide to do or not do something, make it enough of the right thing, and do it on time. Sound judgment leads to good decisions.

One poor judgment increases the probability that another will follow, and as the chain of poor decisions grows, the alternatives for safe flight decrease.

It is possible to break this dangerous poor judgment chain. First, feedback, either from the pilot's senses or an observer, must be received so that a poor judgment can be recognized. Next, a check on stress and anxiety levels is important. High stress causes poor judgment, as we touch on below. Third, problem solving must take place to correct dangerous situations that have resulted from the poor judgment. Fourth, search for other poor judgments, and be sure that the one recognized is the only one affecting the aircraft operation. Last, review the original poor judgments after landing, critically examining them. This, obviously, should help prevent making the same poor judgment again.

Emergencies and Stress

Stress affects judgment and performance. Imagine a bell curve. At the bottom of the scale is sleep, where both judgment and performance are nil. In the center of the bell curve, with stress at a moderate level, one feels challenged, and performance and judgment peak. At the far end, stress causes panic, which brings performance and judgment back to nil. Panic, and the indecision that goes with it, is the most stressful of situations. Therefore, the initial denial or disbelief that there is a problem must be worked through immediately. Then the panic will be put aside and rational thought processes can begin. The challenge is accepted, and control can be taken. Then the pilot can operate within the realms of reactive and rational thinking levels to work through the problem.

Good judgment is worth learning. Pilot error is another term for pilot poor judgment, and it is the biggest cause of aircraft accidents and incidents.

This, and the previous two issues, completes my treatise on attitude and judgment. It is a dry subject, but we all need to think about it on a regular basis.

To complete this issue, I have included a page of Rules of Thumb that I used at the River of No Return Mountain Flying Seminars in Challis, ID. This was the second annual Seminar, and it's a great opportunity for pilots to learn mountain flying techniques, hands on, from some of the best professionals in the business.

Rules of Thumb

1. 1% gradient = 10% change in effective runway length
2. 1% slope = 3% change in landing distance
3. A headwind equaling 1% of landing airspeed will cause 2% decrease in distance (70 with 7 knots wind=10% x 2= 20% decrease in distance).
4. 10 knots tailwind increases stopping distance by 500'
5. 10% speed increase = 20% landing distance increase
6. 50' extra altitude at threshold adds 1000' to landing distance.
7. "Duck-Unders" from 50' adds 4 to 8 knots and up to 400' additional rate of descent
8. Total length of airstrip means little; obstructions can halve the total usable distance.

9. Each 1000' of density altitude increases ground roll of 7 to 8.5%.
10. A 700 fpm climb at sea level becomes 140 fpm at 11000'. At 80 mph, in level terrain, that puts you 315' AGL at 3 miles.
11. An eighth inch of frost increases takeoff distance 50%.
12. To determine runway length: 70 mph x seconds x 1.5 (70 x 12 x 1.5=1260'; use a two-way average in wind).
13. At 80 mph and 1000 fpm, you need 710 horizontal feet for every 100' of obstruction (to clear a 50' obstacle by 50', an additional 1000' of runway is required).

We updated these rules in "Mountain, Canyon, and Backcountry Flying" (Hoover and Williams 2019). And Sherry Knight-Rossiter was one of our expert reviewers on that book.

Winter 1990, Volume 8, Issue 4
Not-So Merry-Go-Arounds

September 1981. North-central Idaho, the Selway Bitterroot Wilderness. A private ranch on the Selway River. One passenger and me in a non-turbo Cessna 206, with half a ton of horse feed, about to land at a challenging airstrip that most pilots, including me, respectfully classify as "one-way."

It not only has a dead end, it has a blind approach. Your final comes after a right turn around a large rock outcropping. Then you can see the short strip immediately in front of you. It ends at the top of a hill, with large trees and two sharp bends in the river upstream.

Years earlier some of the best pros had drilled me: "In wilderness flying, Dick, the first thing to get into your head is that a one-way landing strip has GOT to be a two-way road. The only way out is the way you came in. So never forget the A's and B's of wilderness go-arounds:

A. On a one-way strip, do not attempt to go around, because you will not get there.

B. On a one-way strip, once you get to the no go-around point, you are destined to land. So do it right. You have one chance."

As I said, all that had been drilled into me. But no one had ever told me what to do in a "kill or be killed" situation.

On downwind I scrutinized the strip, and it looked great. The air was cool, not windy. And as we rounded the rocks on short final, I was presented with the undesirable choice I just mentioned: slaughter or suicide. In the middle of the narrow strip, on the touchdown zone, stood the lodge owner with his back to me.

What should I do? Survive, at the probable cost of his life, or seriously jeopardize my passenger and myself by taking an "impossible" alternative? Since then, I've often wondered if I shouldn't have refused to risk two lives to save one.

At that moment, though, the odds must have seemed worth taking, and there was no time for debate. There wasn't even time for a thoughtful obscenity. I firewalled the throttle, selected 20 degrees flaps, and hung on.

Since I'm here to tell the story, obviously at least one person survived. Actually, all three of us did, and so did the plane; but the stall horn probably burned out, after protesting continuously for what seemed like hours. By the time it finally quit, and we were hearing only the comparatively peaceful sound of a strained engine, we were miles upstream. Then we could at last begin to think about a turnaround.

My passenger, an outfitter and veteran flyer, was ashen and shaking so badly he needed an extra half minute to light his cigarette. He asked if I wanted one. He knew I didn't smoke. And I was shaking too much, myself, to accept the offer.

I unloaded the guy at a large airstrip downstream. He had had enough flying for that day (year?). Then I went back to the ranch and the one-way strip. The owner and his wife were abjectly apologetic. They had put a pile of brush out in the runway to keep the horses from rolling in a small wallow there. The woman said, "I thought we were either going to have a squashed husband or a smashed airplane."

"Damn near both," I managed to say.

The episode has haunted me. What would I do next time? I probably could never deliberately choose to kill one man on the chance of saving two others, but I wouldn't gamble again on one-in-a-hundred odds. In that lucky "impossible" go-around, everything just happened to go my way: I made the wrong choice and lived through it. Put in such a predicament again, though, probably I would desperately try to avoid the owner—and would land. I could have landed over the top of him, slammed it on and locked the brakes, and hoped for the best.

Does the episode really apply to Super Cubs? There are several ways of telling yourself that it doesn't:

1. "My plane is a different breed, especially since I've modified it. Practically a helicopter. It will get me out of almost anywhere."

Well, friend, the accident files are full of PA-18s whose pilots attempted go-arounds, failing to accept the difference between "practically" and "actually" a helicopter.

2. "I have always been taught that go-arounds were great. I shouldn't be ashamed to admit making a mistake. I shouldn't be too egotistical to risk losing face, or too bashful to hit the throttle. If I just poured the cobs to her and went around again, I would live to learn from experience. Are you telling me my instructor was crazy?"

Our primary instructors were gods, and always should be. I wouldn't change that. I'm just asking you to know where you are. If you are at the kind of airstrip you learned on, by all means continue to apply your instructor's advice. Do "crash and gos, bounce and bumps, circuits, touchdowns, go-arounds", all the practice things everyone needs to stay current and improve. But if you are in the wilderness, approaching a one-way strip, never forget the two points I began with regarding wilderness go-around.

3. "A smart pilot once told me that every airstrip has a go-around."

I completely agree with that smart pilot, once it's understood that the go-around point on a one-way strip is rarely as late as the final approach. It varies, too, according to plane, load, wind, and other conditions. At the strip where I learned, the go-around point was after touchdown, halfway down the 5000' strip that had no obstructions off the end. On strips I've been to since then, the point may be prior to any approach turns and over 500' AGL.

That agreement brings us back to our first ABCs of backcountry go-arounds. We can add principle C: As you near any challenging strip, decide where the go-around point is going to be. When you are past it, salvage the landing as best you can, and forfeit the airplane to the brush at the end if necessary. If you are unsure of a safe go-around point, plan conservatively, or, better yet, get a check out from a qualified pilot who is already familiar with the landing site.

Go-around accidents are usually horrible. In the Idaho back country an air taxi trying to get out of the wrong smoky canyon crashed with six fatalities. Another attempted go-around caused a stall/spin above the runway, killing all aboard.

I should end with something a little less grisly, a report on an accident scene I was the first to arrive at (a distinction I dread). It looked ghastly. The low-wing Piper had crashed straight ahead into trees off the end, erupting in flames. Miraculously, though one passenger suffered a broken back, all the other occupants escaped serious burning or injury. They had gone in under control, straight ahead, and actually it got to be kind of exciting to watch the fire. The plane had been carrying a lot of hunting ammo, which created some spectacular effects. You'd have thought you were in the neighborhood of a banana republic revolution.

Please be careful and remember the ABCs of backcountry go-arounds.

Unfortunately, the go-around stories continue, usually with bad results. They vary from death and destruction from attempts, to damaged aircraft from over-runs. Which would you prefer?

Spring 1991, Volume 9, Issue 1
Twist and Shout

"Okay, now, power off, flaps up…"

"Power OFF."

I'm afraid I was almost shouting as we twisted down toward terra firma. It was just a routine spin training session, one in which first timers frequently tend to freeze up the first few times around. It becomes a little difficult for instructors to remain calm, cool and professional under those circumstances.

I still do it, though. I am a firm believer in spin training and insist that even my most timid students experience at least a mild entry and recovery before solo. I am convinced that the experience is so far removed from the description that it makes a lasting impression. Granted, unintentional spins from base to final don't allow enough room for recovery. But the knowledge of what spins look and feel like instills a respect that tends to breed care and avoidance.

As a solo student pilot in a Cessna 150 heavy, I could never quite bring myself to do power on stalls, never mind while in a turn. And obtaining the almighty private ticket somehow didn't cure my apprehension about stalls. I was not a Macho Nacho. Just your average beginning flyboy. Eventually, though, as I worked through the ratings and concentrated on improving my flying skills, I became more comfortable with putting airplanes through their paces.

Spins in gliders (sailplanes, to purists), were actually fun, nice and slow and graceful. My powered spin training came from one of those mentors I won't soon forget—

Dwight Blackburn. Dwight was an ag pilot CFI I found after my regular instructor suspiciously never showed up for my CFI required spin training session.

Dwight took it seriously, believing a CFI should not only know recovery from standard spins, but non-standard entries that students can be notorious for.

So after the beads of sweat had faded from straight ahead, no flap, power off entries, we progressed through spin entries slipping over the top, skidding under the bottom, full power, and full flap. It was a workout, but I left Dwight with more confidence than I had ever had before with airplanes.

As a new CFI, I was still a little spooked about taking students through pre-solo spin entry and recovery training, which both my boss and I believed were important, and to this day, I perk right up during spin training.

"Twist and Shout" can go a lot further than scary spin training, though. The shouting can actually be based on pure joy and glee.

One of the most enjoyable hours I ever spent in the air was in an open cockpit Stearman biplane with a competent aerobatic instructor, Hartly Falstead of Chino, Ca. We twisted, shouted, and laughed, dogfighting with another Stearman, trying crazy unnamed maneuvers, just throwing the airplane through the sky to stay out of our opponent's sights, really starting to feel like a part of the airplane.

Now I'm looking forward to more aerobatic training, in some other fun aircraft like a Pitts or Great Lakes.

Fun aside, the benefits of aerobatic training are

substantial. It builds a confidence and ability that can't be learned any other way I've found. It's an important part of aviation. It can get you out of a tight spot. Cubs don't have great aileron control, for example. I've been turned up on a wingtip a couple of times in turbulence. If I ever get tipped up over the top, I want to know how to roll the bird on around.

Of course, aerobatic airplanes are strong and certified for that kind of play. Cubs must be operated at a lower weight and narrower CG envelope to be in the Utility category, which it must be in to do spins. For many Cubs, this means no large people and not much fuel. Other aerobatics, except chandelles and lazy eights, are not allowed in Cubs.

Parachutes are required for aerobatic work. Minimum altitudes (1500' AGL) and clearances (3 miles) apply.

Have fun and be careful out there.

I did continue with some aerobatics, with Bob Hannah in his Pitts, and with the government in OV-10s. I also discovered that many of the popular modifications to Cubs these days prohibit spins, and it is virtually impossible to operate in the utility category with two pilots.

Summer 1991, Volume 9, Issue 2
Time and Money

Time and money—bottom lines, right? Two simple quantities that run our lives, usually on alternating current. If you've got time, you're likely not to have money. And vice versa. This "Murphy's Law Factor" tends to restrict people's pleasure flying. Do I have some spare time? If so, I also seem to have a desk drawer of bills coming due and have to think twice about adding a tab for aviation fuel.

A flying club I once belonged to offered an incentive, an economical benefit: part of a member's monthly dues, two hours' worth, could apply to flying. (Strangely, that nice deal didn't work too well. The idea behind it was safety; helping pilots maintain currency. But with their money problems reduced this way, members would still fall back on the "no-time" excuse).

Your friendly safety columnist has to get tough on once fact of life: if you're going to fly at all, you can't allow yourself to offer or accept any time/money excuse for not staying current. Some things about flying may be like swimming or biking—you never forget them; but there are a lot of special points you do get rusty on if you spend all your time on the ground: numbers, procedures, technical facts, instrument-watching, radio and navigational techniques, just for instance, to say nothing of the "special touch" you develop for that unique set of controls.

We pilots have a commitment of currency to ourselves and our passengers. Rather than pushing the limits of the FARs, fly in the name of safety if you can't find any other reasons! If you don't own an airplane, this is a reason to go and rent one more occasionally. Having a pilot's license carries an ongoing responsibility to keep investing both time and money towards currency and experience—two factors that translate in safety. I'm sorry that many flight instructors fail to drill that point into the heads of primary students. Even if flying is only a hobby, it is like any other hobby in demanding time and money. If you try to settle for halfway measures, though, your hobby of flying can inflict penalties more severe than those of other hobbies.

This month's column focuses on another twosome, the basic flying factors of speed and altitude. When you think about it, flying really boils down to control of speed and altitude. What is slow flight? Speed and altitude. The traffic pattern? Speed and altitude. The approach? Speed and altitude. The landing? Speed and altitude. Get the speed you want, get your altitude where you want it, and the job gets done. Get your speed to stall just as you get your altitude to ground level, and you've done a perfect landing. Have your speed where you want it in the approach with your altitude where it should be, and you have the perfect approach. Sure sounds easy. But really, when you separate the skills involved in flying, it does get easier.

First, practice nailing that airspeed in your everyday flying. Decide what you want for an approach and concentrate on staying on it. Same for threshold speed. 1.3 Vso is 56 at gross in a stock Cub. That's a good speed to start with. 1.1 Vso is 47 at gross—a good target threshold speed for practice. Unfortunately, the speeds at less than gross, or with modified aircraft, largely become a guessing game, hopefully gained by experience with your particular aircraft at altitude.

If we were in a large transport category aircraft, we would go to a set of airspeed tables that would tell us, in relation to our weight and flap settings, a zero-flap speed, an approach and go-around speed, and a threshold speed, and we would have three little bugs to set accordingly on the airspeed indicator. The Twin Otter, for example, has a threshold speed of 70 knots at gross weight, but subtract two thousand pounds and the speed changes to 64 knots. You know how 6 knots of airspeed affects a short field landing! Let's explore that in depth next time.

Unfortunately, there are still pilots out there who like to "add a few knots (indicated airspeed) for grandma and the kids." Do this for wind or turbulence, perhaps, but never just for high altitude airstrips! And don't forget to practice, practice, practice. Today, the best reference for these theories is "Mountain, Canyon, and Backcountry Flying" (Hoover and Williams, 2019). Review, review, review!

Fall 1991, Volume 9, Issue 3
Stall Speeds

We're on final to a short, one-way strip back in Timbuktu. The air is good and solid, and we know we're heavy. We took off at gross weight thirty minutes ago. We've got a helicopter airspeed indicator installed that registers down to twenty mph. we're going to use full flaps, of course, but what are we going to use for an indicated airspeed over the threshold?

Maybe take a wild guess, or just use what feels good? Or, better than that, following the example of a friend who flies out of Nome, slow it down on downwind until the stall horn beeps, and adjust for a percentage above that?

But most older Cubs don't have stall horns, and not many pilots I know would want to slow it right down to the buffet at gross weight on downwind.

As we mentioned last month, large aircraft have approach speeds already calculated out for different weights and configurations. My question, to myself as much as to you, was, why can't we come up with something like that for our Super Cubs? Don't we need that information just as much as the airplane and corporate jocks? After all, we're the ones out in the boondocks flying close to the limits, wanting to get all we can out of our crafts without being dangerous.

My partner, Tim Keogh, and I took our stock wing Cub out (with a 41 Borer prop), to do some testing. Although stall speed (V1 and Vso) are predicated on power off settings, I also wanted to see what indicated stall speeds were with the Borer at full power. We used three different weights—1750, 1525, and 1350. Without recreating the table, I can summarize that the range of speeds went from 45 (no flaps at gross, power off) to 20 (full flaps at 1350# and full power). The next thing we did was calculate approach speeds at 1.3 and 1.1 for normal to very short airstrips, and those varied from 58 to 22 respectively. Looking back, I should have done the second set of stall speeds at a normal power setting for approach, say 1500 rpm, instead of full power for a more useable set of numbers. No one, hopefully, plans to approach at full power! But the point of the exercise should be apparent; you can come up with your own approach numbers for your own personalized airplane, and it should be a pretty good guide during a still air, smooth approach.

Start with 1.3 Vs1 on downwind, and slow appropriately as you configure, all the way to 1.1Vso over the threshold. You already know where it's going to stall power off and power on for your weight. No fuss, no muss, no guess. I like that, assuming the air is solid and calm.

We've always known airspeed control was critical for a good short field landing, but without computing a set of tables for your airplane, with its particular modifications, that critical airspeed control becomes merely a guessing and feeling game.

Unfortunately, with the stock 40 mph airspeed indicator, much of this becomes a guessing game, anyway, unless you opt for an angle of attack indicator. I strongly urge serious short field Cubbers to invest in a helicopter airspeed indicator, and to do a series of stall tests as I have.

We made a similar table to determine loss of altitude during 180 and 270 degree turns after power loss, using different weights, bank angles between 30 and 45, and airspeeds between 55 and 65. We found that we could make 180 turns between 100' and 300', and 270 turns between 200' and 450'. Incidentally, the minimum glider rule after a tow rope break is 200'.

I am *not* advocating using 200' as a minimum to turn back to the airport! There are too many variables at work here, including anticipation, technique, and atmospheric conditions. I am advocating that you go out and do some of this work on your own, in your own airplane, to get to know it and yourself a little better.

But, speaking of angle of attack indicators (AOA), these little jewels can be useful once you get used to them. I have actually flown a Super Cub with one installed. These instruments automatically compensate for different weights by calculating the critical angle of attack of the wing at any given moment, even going through a downdraft. They show the true relationship between angle of attack and stall, and how airspeed is only indirectly related to stall. The adjustment of the instrument is somewhat difficult and critical for accurate readings. They, in and of themselves, are not the only answer to airspeed safety. However, they can be a great pilot aid.

Another airspeed safety "aid" is the aural stall warning. Only the newer Cubs have them, unless added later, and many that have been installed are disconnected. I am convinced that the lack of stall horns on Cubs has contributed to the airplane's poor safety record. I've heard a lot of complaints about them and suspect that many are not adjusted properly. A properly installed and adjusted stall horn is a valuable, even a lifesaving, item. If your experience in Cubs is low, regardless of your other flight experience, consider having one installed on your airplane.

One important thing to remember about the reference speeds is that you still must estimate wind and gust factors, and figure in their effects. The basic recommendation is to add half the gust factor to your airspeed. For example, a 15-knot gust calls for an extra 7 knots or so on the gauge. The other thing is, if we do come up with a table for ref speeds, be sure to experiment with your own airplane, particularly if the wing is not stock, before staking your reputation on the numbers.

Altitude control is a little tough to practice, at least on approach. First, be able to control altitude up high, at different speeds and configurations. For practice choose an altitude and nail it while you change airspeeds and flap settings. When you can do that, pick an airspeed and an altitude and keep them the same while you go from full flaps to no flaps and back and forth.

When practicing approaches, after you can hold an airspeed as desired, constantly evaluate your altitude throughout the approach, making constant small corrections as needed to stay on your desired glideslope. Learning the visual pictures through the windscreen and development of critical depth perception are the keys to altitude control during an approach, and success comes only through practice and more practice. Altitude control, of course, becomes more and more critical the closer you get to the ground. Get that altitude where you want it, when you want it (over the threshold, 1 mph above stall), and you will make a beautiful landing. It's so easy for me to describe, why is it so hard for me to do?

Spend a little time and money in your Cub, and practice control of airspeed and altitude. It will be worth it. Once again, in "Mountain, Canyon, and Backcountry Flying" (Hoover and Williams, 2019), one can find specific suggestions on how to do this.

Winter 1991, Volume 9, Issue 4
FARs and Wingtip Vortices

A whole new FAR Part 91 is on its way out. I think by August or thereabouts it will be effective. We'll try to hit the highlights of it here when the time comes.

The big thing right now for commercial operators and instructors is the new drug testing program. We small operators have to have our testing plans submitted by April 15. The idea behind it is fine, but the implementation is going to completely bog the FAA down. The whole program has not been well thought out, and the idea that sesame seeds, Sudafed, and quinine water can give positive results that could ruin a career has a lot of pilots on the extreme defensive.

What is even more incredible to me is that we actually have pilots flying out there under the influence of alcohol. The awareness of drinking and driving is great these days. Surely pilots understand combining the added dangers of altitude and the third dimension with alcohol. It's deadly. Pure and simple. Suicide and/or murder. And should be treated as such. Let's save the cold beer and the hangovers, for hangar flying.

I had two eye-openers in one flight last week, while coyote hunting. The first was while circling above a coyote waiting for him to come up to better terrain. The wind was dead calm, and in the third circle I must have hit the edge of my wingtip vortices with my left wing. They pulled the left wing down into a steep bank, and I was powerless to pull the wings level. Needless to say, I forgot about the coyote while I tried to figure out if I was losing an aileron or a wing. It only lasted about 4 or 5 seconds, but that feels like a long time when you're 75' off the deck with a hill coming at you.

The second one was the same day, while landing at a nice paved airport with the wind just off the nose at ten or twelve knots. I was doing a flaps up wheel landing, and about 5' off the deck I hit some kind of wind shear or gust, which tipped a wing down violently. Just as I got the wings level, with full power, the bottom dropped out and slammed us to the ground.

I've had really squirrelly winds hit me like that before on landing, probably a half a dozen times in my career. Just enough to remind me never to get complacent about a landing, even if it appears routine. I've hit wing vortices before, too, but never that took control of the airplane that way. It was frightening. Both instances required instant full power and full control inputs.

I suppose that's one thing most of us love about aviation. It's a never-ending learning process, and even a never ending relearning process. But it also gives us an occasional reminder—let's all be careful out there!

Years later we are still talking about the "moose stall," but now there is consideration that it might relate to wing vortices, not just uncoordinated stall/spin scenarios. See "Mountain, Canyon, and Backcountry Flying" (Hoover and Williams, ASA, 2019).

The following is my farewell letter to the SCPA when I was running out of fresh ideas:

Spring 1992, Volume 10, Issue 1
Adieu

This issue's editorial is not a safety column. I'm using it to say adieu, at least temporarily.

You "old timers" may remember my columns beginning back in December 1985. I was spurred on by my love of Super Cubs and the insanity of senseless accidents in them.

Writing the column has been a fun, challenging, and learning experience for me, which I have thoroughly enjoyed.

However, in the same vein as Gary Trudeau (now there's some wishful thinking!), after 44 or so columns, I feel somewhat burned out, drained of interesting items to write about, and mounting pressure from my full-time job that is demanding more and more attention.

I also want to dedicate what spare time I do have to writing an aviation history of Idaho backcountry. Some of the old timers are getting really old, and I want to get their stories down before it's too late.

Jim, of course, has all the rights to my old columns, and is welcome to reprint any of them at his leisure, especially until he replaces me.

I have mixed feelings about dropping this endeavor. I have enjoyed the comradery and new acquaintances that have come my way. Aviators connected to small fabric airplanes are some of the friendliest, most interesting pilots around.

I hate to burn bridges. If Jim will have me back sometime in the future, when my mind is full of fresh and devious Super Cub ideas and time permits, maybe I can once again write some safety columns for the SCPA Newsletter.

Until then, Cubbers, stay in touch, and fly safely out there!

—Dick Williams

There are many cute and humorous aviation quips out there, but this is one of my all-time favorites:

Why I Want to Be a Pilot

I want to be a pilot when I grow up because it's a fun job and easy to do. That's why there are so many pilots flying around today.

Pilots don't need much school, they just have to learn to read numbers so they can read instruments. I guess they should be able to read road maps so they can find their way if they get lost.

Pilots should be brave so they won't be scared if it's foggy and they can't see, or if a wing or motor falls off, they should stay calm. Pilots have to have good eyes to see through clouds, and they can't be afraid of lightening or thunder because they're closer to them than we are.

The salary pilots make is another thing I like. They make more money than they can spend. This is because most people think plane flying is dangerous, except pilots don't because they know how easy it is.

There isn't much I don't like, except that girls like pilots and all the stewardesses want to marry pilots so they always have to chase them away so they won't bother them.

I hope I don't get airsick because I get carsick and if I get airsick I couldn't be a pilot and then I'd have to go to work.

—Essay by a ten-year-old boy

PART 2

✱ ✱ ✱

REBUILDING AND MODIFYING A SUPER CUB AT THE TURN OF THE CENTURY

(photos in Photo Gallery section)

The following prints are from Piper Manufacturing showing some of the original specifications of the aircraft.

Super Cub
PA-18-150 — PIPER

SPECIFICATIONS

ENGINE
H.P. and RPM — Lycoming O-320

WEIGHTS
Gross weight (lbs./kg)
(max take-off/landing) — 1750/794
Standard empty weight (lbs./kg) — 1062/482
Useful load (lbs./kg) — (688/312)

USABLE FUEL CAPACITY (gal./L) — 35.8/135.5

DIMENSIONS
Wing span (ft./m) — 35.3/10.8
Length (ft./m) — 22.5/6.9
Height (ft./m) — 6.7/2

WING AREA/WING LOADING/POWER LOADING
Wing area (ft.^{2}/m^2) — 178.5/16.6
Wing loading (lbs./ft.^{2})/(kg/m^2) — 9.8/47.9
Power loading (lbs/hp)/(kg/hp) — 11.7/5.3

CARGO CAPACITY (lbs./kg) — 50/22.7

PERFORMANCE

TOP SPEED
(kts/mph/kmh) — 113/130/209

CRUISING SPEED
75% power at 5000 ft.
(kts/mph/kmh) — 100/115/185

STALL SPEED
Flaps extended (kts/mph/kmh) — 37/43/69

TAKE-OFF DISTANCE
Take-off run, flaps extended (ft./m) — 200/61
Take-off over 50 ft. obstacle
flaps extended (ft./m) — 500/152

LANDING DISTANCE
Landing roll, flaps extended (ft.m) — 350/107
Landing distance over 50 ft. obstacle,
flaps extended (ft.m) — 885/270

RATE OF CLIMB (fpm/mpm) — 960/292

SERVICE CEILING (ft./m) — 19,000/5791

ABSOLUTE CEILING (ft./m) — 21,300/6492

FUEL CONSUMPTION
75% power (gph/Lph) — 9/34

CRUISING RANGE
75% power (nm/sm/km) — 400/460/741

OPTIONAL EQUIPMENT LIST

VACUUM SYSTEM
Pump, filter, regulator and indicator

INSTRUMENTS
Turn and Bank (electric 3 inch)
Vacuum gyros:
Directional gyro (3 inch)
Artificial horizon (3 inch)
Turn and bank (3 inch)

NIGHT LIGHTING PACKAGE
3 navigation lights
Red tail strobe light
Instrument panel lights
Landing light

AVIONICS
King: KY-97A Comm/Rec
KT-76A Transponder

Narco: Escort II Nav/Comm/Indicator
AT-150 Transponder
AR-850 Encoder

Comm includes microphone, speaker, headset and mike/phone jacks

PIPER
PIPER AIRCRAFT CORP., VERO BEACH, FL 32960

Printed in USA
4-1-88
9995-8-562

Super Cub
PA-18-150 — PIPER

STANDARD/OPTIONAL EQUIPMENT · SPECIFICATION/PERFORMANCE · 1988 STANDARD AIRCRAFT PRICE

SUGGESTED BASE PRICE: $42,595

INCLUDES ALL STANDARD EQUIPMENT
F.A.F. Vero Beach, FL, DELIVERY AND LOCAL TAXES EXTRA

STANDARD EQUIPMENT

POWER PLANT AND PROPELLER
Engine - Lycoming O-320,
 four cylinder, dual magnetos
 150 hp @ 2700 RPM
Crossover exhaust system
Stainless steel exhaust muffler
Carburetor air filter
Carburetor heater shroud
Manual mixture control
Engine oil quick drain
Propeller - Sensenich fixed pitch
 74" diameter metal propeller
Propeller spinner

FLIGHT INSTRUMENTS AND INDICATORS
Airspeed indicator
Sensitive altimeter
Fluid compass
Combination oil pressure and
 temperature gauge

FUEL SYSTEM
36 gallons total; 35.8 usable
 18 gal. wing tanks, two
Header tanks, two
Fuel shut-off valve
Fuel tank sump drains, two
Fuel filter and drain
Electric fuel quantity gauges, two

ELECTRICAL SYSTEM
14v, 60A alternator
Ammeter
12v engine starter
35 amp hr battery
Shielded ignition system

COCKPIT AND FLIGHT CONTROLS
Dual flight controls
Dual brakes
Parking brake
Wing flap control
Cabin heater control
Mixture control
Carburetor heat control
Adjustable fresh air control
Adjustable front seat
Stall warning system

AIRCRAFT FEATURES
High lift metal wing flaps
Sheet metal (aluminum) covered ailerons
Zinc chromate treatment of all
 aluminum parts
Stainless steel control cables
Aerodynamically balanced rudder
 and elevators
Ceconite 7600 covering: fuselage,
 wings and tail surfaces
Upholstered front seat
Upholstered rear seat
Baggage compartment, 18 cu. ft.
Fabric headliner
Seat belts, each seat
Shoulder safety belts, front and rear seats
Cabin heater
Scott 8 in. steerable tail wheel
6.00 x 6; 4 ply tires with rib tread
Tie down rings
Epoxy prime on all steel
 components
Polyurethane finish on exposed
 steel components
12 inch registration numbers
Automatic locator beacon with
 remote switch

Super Cub Owners can select avionics from several options.

Assembly Details

Piper will ship to you all components and hardware necessary to assemble a complete PA 18-150 Piper Super Cub airframe. Cowling, engine baffles, prop spinner and bulkhead, intake airbox, etc., are provided to accommodate a Lycoming 0-320-A2B engine with Sensenich 74" all metal fixed pitch propeller. (Please note: Powerplant and propeller are included only in the optional "engine included" package.)

Fuselage

The Super Cub airframe includes a completely welded and epoxy-primed fuselage frame. Also included are all tail surfaces, landing gear, wheels and brakes, an 8" Scott steerable tail wheel, stainless steel control cables, and standard instrumentation with panel.

Wings

The pre-stamped ribs and pre-drilled fore and aft spars are shipped ready for easy assembly. All necessary compression struts and drag wires are included. The bell cranks are machined. Lift struts are pre-welded and epoxy-primed; insides are pre-oiled.

Fabric Covering

Ceconite 7600 fabric is fire resistant and highly durable. It comes pre-cut and pre-sewn for simple installation as sleeves to fit over fuselage, wings and tail surfaces.

12 Volt Electrical System

For engine starting, a 12 volt electrical system is provided. The system includes a volt meter and all wires prepared ready for installation.

Interior

All closeout panels, floorboards, and seats with pre-sewn covers are included. Interior panels requiring placards are finished in black with appropriate placards in place. Glass window panels and windshield are provided, cut to correct size and contour, ready to install. All prepared fluid lines are formed and flared.

Fuel System

The Super Cub's fuel system consists of two welded 18 gallon wing tanks with two electric quantity gauges and senders, plus all necessary plumbing, including engine primer.

Packaging

You will receive several containers, packaged in sequence, which parallel the detailed step-by-step Piper Owner Assembly Program Manual. An airplane flight manual with weight and balance forms used for completion after assembly, and an airframe log book come with the package.

Hardware

All screws, bolts, nuts, washers, and other hardware needed to complete assembly are included. Each is properly identified.

Pricing

The standard Super Cub Owner Assembly Program Package is priced at **$21,095** F.O.B. Vero Beach, Florida. A complete package including engine and propeller is also available.

For more information, or to order your new Super Cub, call 1-800-72-PIPER

PIPER

Piper Aircraft Corporation
2926 Piper Drive
Vero Beach, Florida 32960

Assemble Your Own Piper Super Cub

With Piper Aircraft's unique Owner Assembly Program you can realize your dream of flying an airplane you had a hand in building. You can of course order a complete factory-built Super Cub from Piper, or you can save substantial cost by assembling it yourself.

And Piper is committed to making it easy for you...every step of the way.

Imagine the joy and profound sense of accomplishment you would feel while flying among the clouds at sunrise in a Super Cub you assembled.

Piper Makes It Easy

We'll ship you all the necessary components, right down to the last nut and bolt. An easy to understand step-by-step Owner's Assembly Manual leads you through the complete assembly process. The tools required are just as simple as those found in a home workshop. No welding, no cutting and no forming are needed.

All of the components necessary to assemble a Piper Super Cub are pre-formed at the factory.

The tubular steel fuselage frame is delivered to you as a single unit, pre-welded and primed. All wing components are pre-formed, ready for assembly. The metal ailerons and flaps are factory-assembled.

The Super Cub's fabric covering is pre-sewn at the factory in the form of sleeves that slip over the fuselage, wings and tail. The lightweight Ceconite 7600 fabric is durable and fire resistant.

The only components not supplied in the standard package are the power plant and propeller. The airframe is designed to accept the reliable 150 HP Lycoming O-320 engine with a 74" Sensenich fixed pitch metal propeller. Piper also gives you the option of purchasing the package complete with new engine and prop from the factory, or if you prefer, you can acquire a rebuilt or used engine elsewhere.

For complete details of the Piper Owner Assembly Program, please see reverse side.

Rebuilding and Modifying a Super Cub at the Turn of the Century

After having flown almost 150 different aircraft makes and models, the Super Cub seems to be one of the most popular to personalize, or as I like to say, "De-Piperize." Heavier, metal aircraft would probably be a little more difficult to modify, even though they are changed to some extent with basic VGs, STOL kits, bigger engines, etc. It is often difficult to distinguish between the modified Cessna 180 and 185 Skywagon, for example. Of the two place fabric airplanes, though, I think the Cub might be so popular because the basic aircraft is such a good, classic design to start with. Even the most drastic certified modifications (larger fuselages, wings, and control surfaces) stick to the basic Cub design. The things that pilots like to change go literally from end to end and tip to tip on this aircraft. Tail surfaces, engines and propellers, wing mods, interiors, utility from agricultural, ski, float, predator control, lumber racks on the belly—the list is unending. One might think of Cub mods in three separate categories: Performance, Safety, and Comfort. The hard-working Cubs of Alaska would naturally favor performance mods and forego most anything for comfort, which usually add weight. Most privately-owned Super Cubs will have several comfort mods, since the cross-country low speed translates to many hours in the saddle.

I believe all should incorporate the safety modifications, and most of them are lightweight. They include, in my opinion, the header-less fuel system (because this eliminates the header tanks and reduces post-impact fire possibilities), the Atley Dodge wing strut reinforcements, the overhead X bar for both seats, shoulder harnesses, the seat belt floor attachment, Vortex Generators, an upgraded gascolator (fire protection) and cargo tie downs.

To me, the Cub is much like the Harley-Davidson motorcycle. They almost beg to be personalized, and most are. It might just be a custom seat or handlebar, or it might be a modified frame and motor. Again, the list is unending.

Back in the days of the Super Cub Pilot's Association at Cub Crafters, Inc. in Yakima, Washington, Jim Richmond's company became the go-to place for Cub modifications. He purchased many of the STC's from Atlee Dodge and Roger Borer and developed more of his own.

You can imagine every Cub pilot, every month, drooling over the changes and improvements he or she might want to incorporate during an annual or a rebuild. My son and I were no exceptions. After teaching my son to fly in our Super Cub in 1998, he went on to the U.S. Air Force Academy and my predator control work was pretty much done. The old working Cub had become a little more than old. It had always been crooked from a poor repair completed before I bought it, but by now it was just becoming an embarrassment to show up in, especially with all the new and beautiful experimental Cubs beginning to exist.

I told my son it was time for the old Cub to belong to someone else. I had always been in aviation as a profession, not a hobby, and did not want to see money going out with nothing coming in. I even put it up for sale officially, albeit briefly, in Jim's newsletter. Meanwhile, my son agreed to buy half interest in the old airplane and help with a complete rebuild. Talk about putting your money where your mouth is!

We decided to go with Steve Tubbs of Performance Air in Caldwell, Idaho, for the reconstruction, with his apprentice John Rogers of Aerocolor, Inc. in Homedale, Idaho, doing most of the work. As an added bonus, my good friend and master craftsman Wayne King was rebuilding his Cub in John's shop and spent many hours helping with ours.

Now we could really start to dream! The first order of business was to disassemble the airplane and send the airframe to the Smith Bros. in Canada, since they owned a jig, were renowned welders, and were already building up experimental Cub fuselages. They ended up replacing about a third of the fuselage tubing due to corrosion and tweaks. Like I said, this was a working Cub!

After a couple thousand hours in Cubs, I already had a pretty good idea what I wanted, but weight was always an issue, and legal options were limited in that day. For example, I would have preferred the 24-gallon Dakota fuel tanks to the larger Atlee Dodge tanks due to price, simplicity, and weight, but they were not certified at the time. However, with care shimming and installing properly, we have never had any cracking or other issues with the large tanks.

Other mods we added later, like the O-360 engine, larger tires, GPS, Rosen sun visor, brake cylinders, and LED navigation and strobe lights, either because they were not available or we simply could not afford them at the time.

Some Interesting Cub Specifications

It's a good idea to review some basic Cub specifications before redesigning the aircraft, to make sure you are moving in the right direction to achieve your goals. New EW and CG ideals are good to keep in mind. Many experienced Cub pilots believe the EW CG should be around 12.25" and the EW itself should be kept under 1,200 pounds to keep the good Cub "feel." It is important to remember that all airplanes, even fighter jets, fly better when they are light.

CG limits for the 2000# GW modification at gross, Normal Category, are 16.2" forward and 20.0" aft. CG limits at gross (1500#) for Utility Category are 12.0" and 19.0".

For the standard Super Cub without the gross weight modification, normal gross limits are 14.0" forward and 20.0" aft. For Utility at 1500#, 12.5 forward and 19.0"aft.

Aileron movement should be 18 degrees or 3 to 5". Elevator movement should be 31 degrees up, 21 degrees down (or 8- 7/16" up and 5" down).

Rudder movement should be 20 degrees left and right, or 7.25". This was amended to 25 degrees for the A model.

Three notch flaps on A models should be set at 20, 37, and 50 degrees.

Thrustline should be less than -1.3 degrees. Factory settings are generally around -4.0 degrees, although with the early technology, it can vary from airplane to airplane. It is harder to see over the nose with this mod, but performance improvement is well worth it.

Elevator gap seals tend to reduce stall speeds up to 7 mph and give the airplane a much more solid feel at slow speed. I call it the "poor man's thrust mod." It does a lot of what the STC does, but with double-sided tape. Since it is easily removable it should not be considered a permanent airframe change in the eyes of the FAA.

The Cub was originally certified under CAR 3, and old standard. Now aircraft are certified under FAR 23, a more stringent standard. Experts say the stock Cub would not pass the 23 standards today.

J.J. Frye of EDO floats states that the Cub has squirrelly directional control on floats because almost half the float is forward of the CG. Stall speed can be 4–5 mph slower on floats because the floats create lift. I have never noticed this "squirrelly-ness".

Bill Rusk, a long time Supercub.org member and experienced re-builder, compiled this list of complete available Super Cub modifications. I have put an asterisk (*) next to the modifications not included in either airplane, and double asterisks (**) next to the modifications included on N2703W but not on N881RW.

 *Reverse Dog Leg (removed)
  Extended Baggage
 *Metal Belly
  Removable Rear Seat Cross Bar
  Cargo Tie-downs
  Bushed Tailwheel Attach bolt—reinforced area
  Float Fittings
  Float Lift Rings
  Dual Tail Lift Handles

Firewall X Brace
Cabin Roof X Brace
Extended Gear
Heavy Duty Gear (how old is the gear?)
Seat Belt Floor Attachment versus On The Seat
X Brace at Turtle Deck Above Lifting Handles
Welded Tubes versus Stringers
Inertial Reel Shoulder Harness set up
Flap Handle Mods—notches
* Long Step—Gear Bushed for Long Step
* Extended Front Seat Attach Tabs
ELT Mount and Model
Tail X Brace
3rd Seat Reinforcement/STC
* Extended Stick
* Folding Front Seat
* Control Lock
Parking Brake
Tail Stinger Light
Extended Baggage Door
* Upper Cargo Bay
* Metal Headliner
* AOSS Gear
* Slotted/Slatted Wing
VG's
Tanks: 18/24/30
Header-less Fuel System
** Square Wing Tips versus Round Wing Tip
** Square Tail Surfaces versus Stock
Bushwheels
Double Puck Brakes

Thrust Line Mod
Flaps Extended Inboard
Defroster
Rear Seat Heat
* Left Window Slider, Fixed, Folding
Heavy Duty Lift Struts (AD Compliance)
Avionics
Paint Scheme and Quality
   (fabric over 30 years old is suspect)
Empty Weight
Borer Prop
* Engine Heater
* Primer to 1 Cylinder or All Four
Mag Type and Age
Battery Location (under seat)
* Fish Pole Tube
Wig Wag Lights
Muffler Upgrade and Condition
Lightweight Starter and Alternator
Safety Cables on Gear
Atlee Spar Reinforcement/Tie down
2000Pd Gross Weight Mod
Under seat Storage Box
LED Strobe Lights
Upgraded Gascolator
* Extended Leading Edges
* Dual Door
Brake Boosters/Upgraded Brake Master Cylinders

The Rebuild Story

The first big decision during this process was whether or not to stay certified. In 2000, the experimental Cubs were just starting to appear and no one really knew at that time how that was going to work out. As it turned out, they are wonderful. But I saw a certain value in owning a certified Cub, since there seemed to be less out there every week, and no more were being made. In the end we decided to stay certified, and I'm still not positive it was the best decision. It certainly wasn't the best monetary decision, as we spent over $20,000 on 29 STCs, and tons of paperwork on another 17 337 FAA Field Approvals. We were one of the last aircraft to easily get Field Approvals, and probably the only certified Cub with carbon fiber interior panels, as the FAA was changing its mind about field approvals and severely limiting them.

Keep in mind that the certified and experimental worlds are very different. Often the experimental world will leak over to the certified, however. Avionics are a good example of this, as they get TSO'd and certified. Another example is propellers. Sensenich just recently got their ground-adjustable propeller certified for Cubs, with a reported 15+ knot increase in groundspeed. The worlds are ever changing.

N881RW, formerly N8480H, is a PA-18A built in 1957, serial number 18-6627. The "Ag" model had several structural modifications from the factory and was certified under the Restricted Category at a gross weight of 2070 pounds. A few of these mods included:

- A hopper door aft of the rear wing fittings
- Removable rear seat
- Rudder travel increased to 25 degrees right and left
- Re-routed flap cables
- Fuselage structure strengthened for rear seat load of 230 pounds
- Metal belly
- Hopper tank and lid
- Corrosion proofed fuselage

I was tired of the "sway back" look so we put the straight 18 "turtle deck" on. With removal of the metal belly, hopper, old radios and wiring, etc., we took 70 pounds off. By adding the Atley Dodge fuel tanks, heavier 3" gear, Bushwheels, and miscellaneous comfort items, we added 40 pounds back on, for a net loss of 30 pounds. The total Empty Weight and CG on this aircraft came to 1175 and 11.4".

Modification Explanation

Engine

Lycoming O-360C4P, ported and flowed by Lycon Corporation. This is Cub Crafters STC SA92NW and includes new cowling. Porting and flowing adds about 5 horsepower per cylinder but is not included with the STC. Conical engine mount.

Propeller: The McCauley 1A200 and a Sensenich model are both approved propellers for the Cub 180 hp STC conversion. But the preferred propeller is the McCauley 1P235 used on the Pawnee and often called the "Borer 180 prop" and used on many experimental Cubs. The O-320 Borer prop is the McCauley GM8241-44. The FAA used to do field approvals (337s) on the McCauley FA 8452 but stopped since testing had not been done with the PA-18. There are several other available propellers (mostly for the experimental) including the Sensenich WC-80 composite, Catto, Scimitar MT, and the constant speed Hartzell Trailblazer. Ground clearance becomes an issue with many of these props without extended gear or large tires.

Exhaust: Performance Air Motive (PAMI) Exhaust STC SA02273AK. With this engine and exhaust, Lycon dyno-tested the horsepower at 212.

Thrustline Products STC SA02211AK. Plugs lift the engine thrust line to close to zero for improved performance in almost every aspect, particularly on floatplanes.

Brackett Air Filter STC

Nippondenso Lightweight Alternator. As with the starter, lighter is better.

SkyTech Lightweight Starter, STC SE00218NY.

BC Oil Filter: It has always seemed strange to me that stock Cubs had no filter, just a screen. I feel a lot better with a filter, and it stretches the time between oil changes.

Oil/Fuel Separator: We added this because I was tired of oil on the belly. This definitely helped, but the dirty oil is held outside the engine, not returned inside.

Fuel

Steve's Aircraft gasolator STC SA01026SE. Solid brass to decrease rupture possibility during impact.

Atley Dodge 60-gallon fuel tanks STC SA649AL. Adds 11 pounds, but the stock 36 gallons is just not enough.

"Both" Fuel System, Cub Crafters STC SA00415SE. This, along with eliminating the header tanks, saves weight, decreases risk of fire and tank rupture, and simplifies the system.

Jensen Fuel Valve STC SA1554NM, improvement over stock.

Vented fuel caps, Atlee Dodge STC SA02040AK

Instruments

Electronics International Tachometer STC SA924NM. Accurate and lightweight engine recording.

Electronics International fuel flow gauge STC SA00068SE. Needed with large fuel tanks as the old gauges don't give you enough information at the low end. Extremely accurate when calibrated correctly.

Gear

Dakota master cylinder brakes STC SA02234AK. Along with double-puck Cleveland Brakes and high-pressure lines, braking is dramatically improved.

Bushwheels STC SA01015SE. These 31" tires dramatically improve soft field performance.

Baby Bushwheel STC SA01233SE.

Atlee Dodge gear cables STC SA4606NM. These safety cables will prevent complete failure in the event of a cabane failure.

3" Gear Extension, Cub Crafters STC SA00411SE. Better angle of attack and ground clearance.

Atlee Dodge Float Fittings, STC SA4615NM. Weld on. Do it when the fabric is off regardless of future plans.

Abrasion Tape on leading edges to help prevent paint chipping from rocks.

2-hole tailwheel attach. This is much stronger than the single hole for rough terrain.

Fuselage

Atlee Dodge front seatbelt attach STC SA02043AK. This is a critical safety item, basing the belt attach to the floor instead of the seat.

Wipaire STC SA00997CH, Gross Weight Increase to 2000#, Landplane. An increase from 1750#.

Third Seat, Roger Borer STC SA5-7 and SA5-29. In the A Model this allows a weight increase from 50# to 170# and adds a seatbelt without additional structure. Child's seat and/or more baggage weight.

Atlee Dodge top deck tubing STC SA02011AK. This converted the "flat back" to the "turtle deck".

Poly-fiber fabric STC SA 1008WE. Stitts.

Cub Crafters map pocket. 337 Field Approval. Just handy.

Lower entrance door Plexiglas cover, field approval. Nice to have for increased visibility.

Rear fuselage ground handling receptacle, field approval. Nice to have, particularly on skis.

Atley Dodge Cross Brace over Pilot Seat, STC SA02011AK. Mandatory for crash protection, and available for the rear in non-A models.

Aluminum floorboards, field approval. Saves some weight. Rear seat back aluminum, hinged. Field approval, weight-saver and ease of loading.

Cub Crafters under seat storage, field approval.

Rear Seat Crossbar, hinged. Field approval. Handy for aft baggage loading.

Large baggage compartment, field approval. Removes the dogleg.

New Instrument Panel, field approval. Clean-up.

Dan's Aircraft Light Battery STC SA0213AK. Better CG, less weight.

Top Deck Skylight, field approval. Handmade by Wayne King.

Inertial Reel Shoulder Harnesses, 5 point, front and rear, Am Safe.

LED Strobe/Nav Lights.

Rear seat heater/defroster. Field Approval.

Rosen Sun visor, STC SAO1251SE.

Carbon Fiber Interior Panels, field approval.

Wings

Landing Light Pulse light STC SA4005NM. Improves visibility and lengthens bulb life.

Cub Crafters Vortex Generators STC SA000275SE. The flight characteristic improvements of these are well known.

Atlee Dodge front lift strut bracket STC SA02026AK. A critical inexpensive wing strengthener.

Inboard flap extensions, field approval. Cleans up the wing roots, slight performance increase.

Fueling Steps. I like the small ones, not the large long one.

Elevator Gap Seals.

The Third Seat Story

Although the third seat STC was primarily to up the baggage load limit and carry a child in a car seat, a small adult can squeeze in for a short ride if claustrophobia is not an issue. My partner, Tim Keogh, once sat back there from the backcountry to Boise, with the FAA sitting in the middle seat! That was, of course, after we had showed him the paperwork and weight & balance.

My son obtained his Private Pilot License during his senior year in high school and proposed taking his prom date (and her friend!) for a picnic ride early on prom day. To my astonishment, the girls' parents agreed.

As Patrick was fueling at the local airport, the manager came out to question and accuse him of being illegal and overweight with two passengers. My son, intimidated and flustered, called me after failing to convince this blowhard. I was there in less than thirty minutes to set the manager straight, and my son and his "girlfriends" had a nice little outing after all.

N2703W

In 2019, my son Patrick purchased Wayne King's "King Cub". Wayne had rebuilt this Cub during the same timeframe we were doing ours, with Steve Tubbs' oversight. It is interesting to note the different modifications on this aircraft. We call it "The Square Cub" because the instrument panel, wings, and tail are squared off, giving it slightly more wing area.

The Empty Weight and CG on this aircraft are 1150 and 11.84".

This airplane was originally an Italian L-18C Serial Number 51-15306, with a Continental C90 engine and a manufacture date of 1982, which seems incorrect and was probably updated when converted to a PA18. It was upgraded to the PA-18 GW of 1750. One old piece of paperwork calls it a PA-19.

Alex Clark explains on Supercub.org:

There were two types of L 18s. The L-18B was a PA-11-90 Cub Special with military L4J windows. There were about 105 built.

The L-18C was a PA-18-95 with military modifications. Piper originally called these PA-19s. But, they changed their minds after about three aircraft had been built as PA-19s and then they decided to call the PA-19 a PA-18 variant. About 840 L-18Cs were produced (Wayne's was Italian).

The PA-18-95 (L-18C) was the first series of Super Cubs. They have more and different tubing. The original empty weight was around 800 to 840 pounds. The gross weight was 1500 on wheels, originally with no flaps. It originally had one 18-gallon fuel tank in the left wing. The original tail surfaces were smaller than the 150 horsepower models.

And Alex explained further in a more recent note to me:

Howdy from Homer, Alaska.

As I am sure you probably already know, the L-18Bs were PA-11 Cub Specials that were military versions.

Then they decided to try using the newer PA-18-95 Super Cubs for military purposes. The military called them "L-18Cs."

For some reason, Piper initially thought that they would designate the military version of the PA-18-95s, (L-18Cs) as PA-19s.

Well that did not last long (only three planes I think) and they just started calling them PA-18s after only three had true PA-19 serial numbers. But you see PA-19 listed on FAA and Piper Paperwork so those three planes will always be included and anything good enough for them is also good enough for a PA-18 and vice-versa.

The Air Force bought around 839 L-18Cs between 1950 and 1953. About 108 to 110 of them were sent to allied countries under the Military Defense Assistance Program (MDAP.)

Italy received 20 L-18Cs and also about 62 later L-21Bs (PA-18-135s)

In 1951 the serial numbers for L-18C Military Super Cub 95 is from 51-15272 to 51-15329.

I would bet a hamburger that your 1982 registration comes from the year it was reassembled or rebuilt after being imported back into the USA as a pile of parts.

I helped rebuild one back around 1991 and that former Italian L21B now has a 1991 air worthiness cert.

Alex Clark
Dragonfly Aero
Homer, Alaska

As it turns out, my friend Brian Dunlop (*Notes From the Cockpit*, 2015) has even more interesting L19 information to add. He says: "My type data certificate (a US one) said PA19 as well as PA18. The serial numbers were only four figures. Mine was 18-1553. All had the greenhouse glass and not the rounded rear one.

My PA19 was a French one and they had around 350 supplied under the Marshall Aid Plan as did the Dutch, Italians, Greeks, and Israelis.

There were a few kept back in the US and I have seen one at the Aberdeen Proving Grounds in MD used by the flying club.

I found mine in Belgium with a civil registration. I towed it to the ferry (on its wheels and with the wings strapped to the side of the fuselage!!) with a Volvo and then from Dover to my home behind my 1964 Fairlane wagon that once belonged to Ringo Starr.

My airplane had a normal Super Cub fuselage with brackets and holes in the rear spar for flaps, but no flaps.

My airplane had 36 gallons of fuel. Some were even fitted with bazookas...these were attached above the struts outboard of the cabane struts with a wire to pull when required!!

No electrics at all although they fitted a large army radio in the back behind the seat with a long whip antenna out of a hole in the greenhouse roof. To power it they fitted a truck generator on the top front of the C-90-8 with a belt drive to a pulley fitted behind the prop and then a huge non-aerodynamic flat fronted hump to cover it."

Engine

These are identical mods to N881RW except for the exhaust system and a slightly different alternator. It does not have an oil separator.

- Professional Pilots Inc. (formerly Grumman Sutton) Exhaust STC ST01920CH
  Thrustline STC SA02211AK
- McCauley Propeller STC SA92NM. This is the 1A200-FA8242. Experimental owners generally prefer the IP235 78" "Borer" style prop, or the FA8452 Pawnee Prop that the FAA used to approve on a 337.
- Sky Tech Model 122-12LS Lightweight Starter STC SA92NW
- Oil Cooler as per Engine STC SA92NW
- Lycoming O-360-C4P STC SA92NW
- B&C Alternator 40 amp, STC SA02183AK
- Steve's fuel gasolator STC SA01026SE

Gear

The brake master cylinder is a different one from N881RW, as well as the AOSS gear.

- Cleveland Wheels & Brakes Model 199-71
- Alaska Bushwheel 31" Tires STC SA01015SE
- Bushwheel Tailwheel 2 Hole Univair Tailspring
- Parking Brake Installation
- Cub Crafters 3" Extended Gear STC SA00411SE
- Steve's SA6-01 Master Cylinder STC SA01516SE
- Float Fittings STC SA4615NM
- AOSS gear, replacing the old bungee system.

Electrical

- Precise Flight Pulselite landing lights STC SA4005NM
- Lightweight Battery
- LED Strobe/Nav lights

Interior

Except for some instrument and radio differences, and Cub Crafters seats, the interior is very close to N881RW.

- EI Fuel Flow
- EI Oil pressure/Temp
- EI Carb/OAT gauge
- EI Digital Volt/Amp Gauge
- Inertial Reel Shoulder Harnesses Am Safe
- Jenson fuel valve plug STC SA1554NM
- Top Deck X Brace Atley Dodge STC SO2011AK
- Hinged Crossbar
- Folding back seat
- Map pocket
- Underseat storage

- Extended baggage STC SA00388NY
- Fuel system "both" Cub Crafters STC SA00415SE
- Extended skylight
- Plexiglass bottom door
- Intercom PM 1000
- AmeriKing AR-350 Encoder
- Amerex Fire Extinguisher, Halon 1211
- Garmin GNC250XL SPS/Comm
- King KT76A Transponder
- Davtron M800 Clock
- Square Instrument Panel STC SA00572SE
- Side Access Door STC SA0070SE Cub Crafters
- GW Increase to 1750# Borer STC SA292AL

Wings

The square tips and extended ailerons are differences from N881RW.

- BLR VGs STC SA00275SE
- Flush Flap STC SA490AL
- Square Wingtips STC SA460SW
- Square Tail STC SA589AL
- Extended Ailerons STC SA612AL
- Poly-Fiber STC SA1008WE

We consider 03W the better flying machine. It is lighter and the extra wing surfaces seem to make a difference.

PART 3

***

ZEN AND THE ART OF BACKCOUNTRY FLYING: AN ESSAY

(photos in Photo Gallery section)

Introduction and Background

In 1974, Robert Pirsig wrote a classic called *Zen and the Art of Motorcycle Maintenance*. Shortly thereafter he stated that the book should "in no way be associated with that great body of factual information relating to orthodox Zen Buddhist practices. It's not very factual on motorcycles either." He also said, "The motorcycle is mainly a mental phenomenon…A study of the art of motorcycle maintenance is really a miniature study of the art of rationality itself."

As I read "Zen" for the second time, with backcountry flying in mind, I realized that many parallels could be drawn between the motorcycle and the backcountry airplane, as well as the important mental processes needed to cope with both at the expert level.

Let's start with some definitions from Wikipedia. Zen has been described as "a state of calm attentiveness in which one's actions are guided by intuition rather than by conscious effort" (Irene Virag). Another definition says it is "being one with the activity, to engage in it fully, to see and appreciate the most minute detail in it…"

These are the goals to keep in mind as we discuss Zen in terms of specialized backcountry flying, because relating the flying to that level will increase the **art** and **safety** of the activity.

Backcountry flying can be defined as the aspect of fixed-wing aviation in which operations take place on unimproved airstrips, often with non-standard approach and departure procedures and where STOL techniques are often the norm.

Pirsig discusses several terms and activities in his

book, and these are worth relating and comparing to backcountry aviation.

For example, one concept Pirsig plays with is Quality, which he describes as "the knife edge moment of grasping something before thinking about it." This is definitely part of being one with the aircraft while approaching a critical airstrip, and if you are reading the book or watching YouTube video on an approach just before actually flying it, you are not operating with "quality"! We have actually found wrecked airplanes on backcountry airstrips with a "how to" book describing the approach open in the front seat.

The author also talks about "ego-climbing" versus "selfless climbing" during the ascent of a mountain, but the word climbing could easily be replaced with the words "backcountry flying." This is a common problem, particularly in "gaggle" flying, as it is a natural instinct to keep up with your buddies or prove something to yourself. Ego really does not have a safe place in backcountry flying. Pirsig says that mechanics (and pilots, I've found) tend to be rather modest and quiet, and skeptical as well when it comes to weather and airstrip reports. He also talks about expert mechanics developing a feel, for example, discerning the subtle differences between finger tight, snug, and tight. It reminded me of the feel a pilot develops doing this kind of flying: a sub-conscious control touch, light and sensitive, sensing the airplane, the air, and the movement of the machine through that air. It is another valuable skill the backcountry pilot needs.

Pirsig explores the differences between art and technology, very similar to Beryl Markham in *West with the Night*. Science and Art are one, he says. Markham describes it eloquently, saying that the two must work together to become one. This holds a huge truth for backcountry aviation. While pilots need to understand and master the technology of aviation, the backcountry requires a higher level of mastery where the art is recognized and strived for. The pilot's actions must be subconscious, smooth, and accurate for successful backcountry flying. Paul Claus, an Alaskan bush and glacier expert, describes it well in *Mountain, Canyon, and Backcountry Flying* (Hoover and Williams, 2019).

And for technology, Pirsig says "The Buddha, the Godhead, resides quite as comfortable in the circuits of a digital computer or the gears of a cycle transmission as he does at the top of a mountain or in the petals of a flower." Replace "gears of a cycle transmission" with "the cylinders of an aircraft engine," and you get the connection.

When Pirsig talks about mechanics, he states, "You can't really think hard about what you're doing and listen to the radio at the same time." He is talking about distractions, a fatal flaw in both aircraft flying and maintenance. Lenny Skunberg, a master mechanic, addresses this in *Mountain, Canyon, and Backcountry Flying* (Hoover and Williams, 2019). Also, psychologists now widely agree that multi-tasking is a myth and cannot be maintained for any length of time. Don't try to do it while you are involved in backcountry flying. Here is a link to an interesting in-depth article on the subject: *https://ojs.library.okstate.edu/osu/index.php/CARI/article/view/7565/6966*

Pirsig says, "Slow down and be involved, not detached. When you want to hurry something, that means you no longer care about it and want to get on to other things." This is worth thinking about. This is an easy trap for a pilot to fall into, especially a pilot flying for a living. An old sage and I were both working for a backcountry charter service once, and management was notorious for always being behind and pushing the pilots to catch up.

As soon as the pressure was put on, this old master would intentionally slow down to about half speed. He counseled me that going too quickly was a dangerous trap that would result in damage and tragedy. And he was right.

I like what Pirsig has to say about the personality of a machine. He described it as the intuitive sum total of everything you know and feel about it, and also how you treat it. I think most pilots can relate to this in regard to their own airplane and what they know and feel about it. We know that the machine will often "talk" to us and try to tell us how it is feeling. In the backcountry, in remote terrain with few landing areas, this is a critical relationship for a pilot to have with his craft. A "Oneness," you might say.

In speaking directly about motorcycle maintenance, Pirsig says that "Peace of mind produces good maintenance. If you don't have this when you start and maintain it while you're working you're likely to build your personal problems right into the machine itself." I could also argue that good maintenance produces peace of mind, but this is something to keep in mind regarding both you and your airplane mechanic. I think most of us would agree that a mechanic who is in a hurry or has other distractions on his mind is likely to miss something or do something sloppy on your airplane. I, in fact, have seen this happen. And it is the same for us as pilots flying the machine. Being in a hurry can be the kiss of death for both mechanics and pilots.

Robert Pirsig writes quite a bit about issues having to do with working on a motorcycle, but they can be likened to issues flying a backcountry airplane too. He says that at times motorcycle maintenance can get frustrating, even infuriating, but that is part of what makes it interesting. This can certainly be true in the demands of backcountry flying. Sometimes it just doesn't feel right and you can't get "in the groove." Pirsig recommends slowing down, thinking about it, even stopping and resting for up to a month.

This is all good advice for the pilot. Sometimes trying to force an issue will result in aircraft damage or worse. Chill for a while and regroup. Let your mind settle a bit.

A Backcountry Flight

Notes From The Cockpit told the stories, and *Mountain, Canyon, and Backcountry Flying* told the how-to, but what about the actual in-flight thought processes that go into a backcountry flight? We know the generalities about pre-flight planning, preparation, risk management, and decision-making, but what is going on in an experienced pilot's head before, during, and after a challenging backcountry flight?

Let's take a look.

The Night Before

There is an airstrip in the Idaho backcountry that used to be called Simplot, which was the owner's name. The name has changed, as well as the length and condition, but when I began flying it, it was 900' long for landing, 1000' for takeoff, at 4000' elevation with no go-around. I have operated Super Cubs, C-182s, C-185s, C-206s, C-207s, Islanders, and Twin Otters on this airstrip, and consider the C-207 the most challenging aircraft to operate there. This is primarily due to its increased empty weight and CG range from the 206, and also because of its limited flap range. Although the Twin Otter is intimidating on such a small strip because of its size, after you get used to it the only aircraft I've found easier to operate there is the Super Cub. The 185 was next in difficulty to the 207 because of its ability to bounce and the fact that we operated at max weight with a belly pod. The heavy 185 at the aft CG limit is a completely different animal than a light aircraft with center CG. I've often thought that STOL competitions should be conducted at gross weight to more accurately simulate what professionals do. That would be real world. Any aircraft I have flown, from a Cub to a jet, flies better when it is light.

Flying an airplane near its performance and weight limit into a difficult airstrip is much like using a very sharp knife. The sharper the knife, the easier the job. The problem with a super sharp knife is that it tends to lose that edge quite quickly. It is the same with the sharp pilot. When he or she is very sharp, the task is easier and not nearly as stressful. And the pilot stays very sharp when he is doing that task almost every day. But what happens when he hasn't operated there for, say, two weeks? That sharpness is gone, and hopefully the pilot is still sharp enough to realize it. Realize it! A pilot loses proficiency in a couple of weeks in this regime.

Generally, something the night before will remind him. As the flight is reviewed in his mind, there might be a slightly accelerated heartbeat, a slight case of nerves. This will probably cause him to really think about the flight, the approach, the landing, and the takeoff. He will relate it directly to the aircraft he will be flying, and although some nervousness might remain, visualizing the familiar procedures will most likely alleviate much concern.

If it doesn't, don't worry yet, the flight hasn't even begun!

Of course, the usual weather factors are being considered for this flight. Any frontal activity, instability, wind, or heat, is going to scrub this flight immediately. Right?

The Morning Of

The pilot may or may not have slept well. I find this is usually not an issue, as there will be enough adrenaline flowing to retain consciousness and alertness. Another check of the weather puts the mission on go status. There may be some lingering nervousness. That's ok. Complacency, however, is not (unless perhaps it is feigned, to mask the nerves for the passengers). By the way, if you are taking an instructional flight, be aware that your instructor may be going through similar emotions and thoughts. For this example, we are assuming this is not a first-time flight. This is a flight where you consider yourself somewhat less than super-sharp but have done it before.

The fuel and cargo load go through a final consideration.

The Flight

The pilot immediately begins sensing the elements. The aircraft behavior, the air, and himself. Aircraft, smooth? Air, smooth? Pilot, smooth?

And this continues, consciously and subconsciously, until arrival.

At arrival, over the airstrip, any remaining nervousness will generally disappear. You've done this before, perhaps many times, and your senses have not picked up any negative vibes. You are back, and you settle in for the job at hand.

If, however, that nervousness won't go away, or it gets worse, it's time to re-evaluate. What's going on? Can you identify what doesn't feel right? It may be nebulous, but that doesn't mean you should ignore it. If you are with an instructor/check pilot, tell him. Talk about it. Try to get to the bottom of it. And if you can't get rid of it, or figure it out, it is time to go home or somewhere else. Do not ignore your sixth sense, just because you don't understand it!

If you're flying in a gaggle, you have a whole different set of issues. Geese fly in gaggles, and they do a good job of it. They know each other intimately, their flying skills are probably virtually equal, and they have the same goal in mind.

A bunch of pilots flying together in a gaggle, however, is a different thing. Different egos, different goals, different skills, different currency, and probably different mindsets, since humans have more brain power than geese (we assume).

I like to fly in some gaggles when the pilots know each other very well and certain understandings are in place, and the maximum is usually five, but not in populated areas like the Idaho backcountry in the summer. Otherwise, three would be a normal maximum and four an exception. Anything larger has too much potential for problems. If someone doesn't like a landing spot he circles overhead or goes to another place, no questions or comments made. It could be he is capable of the landing but just doesn't feel like it that day. No problem. No ego. No pressure.

But all too often that is not the case. There are egos involved, and the pressure is on, self-inflicted or not, to measure up. It can be an invitation to disaster, and I've seen it happen.

Be cautious with your thought processes when flying in a gaggle!

I was responsible for a gaggle during a fly-in in the early days of the SCPA, described early in Part 1. There were probably about 15 or 20 of us, and we started at Sulphur Creek. An old timer from Wyoming, by himself, made a go-around from the lodge area, similar to the accident in 2020 in a 182. This guy made it around, somehow, by the skin of his teeth.

Another unforgettable gaggle story occurred about 40 years ago at Indian Creek. During a very busy time for air taxi pilots supporting whitewater rafting, a large group of low wing Pipers came in without any organization or leadership. Some were on the wrong frequency. Others were calling downstream upstream and vice-versa. The air taxi pilots in the air wisely pulled away and circled until things settled down and the professionals already on the ground helped with some guidance.

Personally, I prefer one airplane with one student while instructing in the backcountry. If we have two airplanes, depending on the difficulty of the airstrip, I will put the student in the back of my airplane first and show him the approach, landing, and departure. Then, if we agree, we will take the student's airplane with me as instructor. I have allowed another airplane to accompany us if I know the pilot and his qualifications.

The Approach and Landing

Field condition. Airspeed and Altitude. Key positions in the approach. Abort points. Small corrections. Wind. The feel and sound of the airplane. And the pilot. How am I doing? Am I "on?" Abort points. Aim point. Wind. Airspeed and Altitude. Constant small corrections. Touchdown: be ready for instantaneous correction for bounce, gust, malfunction. Brake. Taxi carefully.

Departure

Strip condition. Wind. Departure path for bad air and emergencies. Air. Load. Emergency Options. Lift-off point. These things change constantly and are constantly evaluated. I remember talking with another air taxi pilot at an airstrip in the wilderness. We were trying to evaluate departure loads with the current temperature and wind, and finally agreed on two or three passengers and very little baggage, but the changing conditions really had us scratching our heads and working together on it.

The Return

Recently I was on a return trip from Boise to Salmon and encountered something I'd never seen before in all my experience. It was windy at 10,000', and I had opted against a landing at Sulphur Creek on the way due to some tailwind on the surface. As I crossed the high ridge a few miles east, I got a pretty good licking. I climbed way higher than normal, almost 11,500', to get away from the mountain ridge turbulence. Then, only about 30 miles from Salmon, I saw a large lenticular cloud form out ahead of me, and it was mesmerizing, startling, and almost unbelievable. It was right in my path and moving toward the summit I had planned to descend from.

I was initially in denial. It was just hard to believe it was happening. But I eventually realized this was a real, and serious, thing, and I was going to have to deal with it in a way not ever required before. I turned north to a point that would put me about 20 miles north of Salmon for a descent, watching it very closely as I circumvented it and it continued to morph before my eyes. Sure enough, it went right over that summit and began tearing itself to pieces where there are always significant downdrafts. My descent to the north was rough but not horrible. But the flight left me with the thought that one is still learning, and seeing new things, after all that experience—and I had better be ready to act and react to something entirely new at any time.

Expanding the Senses

Take your sight and expand it peripherally and behind you. Look behind you en-route for escapes and developments, and peripherally when on short final and roll-out, for game and unforeseen obstacles.

Take your ears and expand them to listen to your engine and immediate surroundings, even with your noise-cancelling headsets on. And maybe to what your friends are trying to tell you.

Take your touch, and expand it to feel your stick, yoke, pedals, throttle, and brakes. Have a light enough touch to sense whatever you're touching is trying to tell you, as well as what you are trying to tell it.

Expand the taste in your mouth. That dry cottonmouth is worth paying attention to. Even when it is telling you to drink a cold beer when you're done flying!

Pay attention to your sense of smell. Your airplane might be talking to you. Or maybe your body.

Proprioception is the sense of your brain knowing where your body is. This is hand-eye coordination, and I've found it to be one of the key skills of great pilots.

Synesthesia allows some people to associate sounds as colors or sights as smells, for example. I am not familiar with it or any pilots who have that ability, but it would be fascinating.

And then, of course, what we call the Sixth Sense. That haunting, quiet, off-to-the-side nagging feeling that can't be identified. Maybe a feeling of foreboding or angst, quite easy to ignore and dismiss because it is so intangible. Maybe there's something to it, maybe there's not. Maybe a waste of time to pay attention to. Maybe not.

Lapses of the Senses

Obviously, we are more in tune with our senses at some times over others. Develop the self-awareness to know when you are on your game and when you are not. This is sometimes called Biorhythms. Be aware that your rhythms will rarely be the same or in tune with others around you.

Single Pilot Operations

I spent my first 7,000 hours as a single pilot operator with no autopilot. Although I talked to other pilots on the radio and on the ground, I got very used to doing things on my own.

It was a pleasant change to fly twin-engine turboprops with another pilot, particularly ones with more experience than myself. CRM was a young and undeveloped concept at the time, but the safety advantages of two pilots was immediately obvious.

As CRM developed and the aircraft I flew became more complex, the advantages of a good two pilot crew really came into their own. There was clear division of duties with one pilot always flying the airplane both in normal and emergency operations. When executed properly, two-pilot crews are definitely the way to go for safety and efficiency.

But now, as a retiree, I am back to single pilot operations. And while I enjoy the solitude and freedom being alone in the cockpit, it has given me a chance to re-evaluate both types of flying.

You are alone as a single pilot, with no one really to talk to. Oh, you have the radio, and a lot of time is spent teaching us how to communicate with that device to our best advantage regarding help, but it is just not the same as someone in the cockpit with you to discuss options and scenarios as they play out. In some ways, the single pilot remains at a distinct disadvantage to a crew of two or more. Professional flight departments have other kinds of safety and communication resources, too, such as Safety Management Systems (SMS) and formal pre-flight risk assessments. A good professional flight department develops an entire culture built around good safe operating practices and standard operating procedures (SOPS). Airlines limit their crews to certain airports and procedures until the proper training has been met. This is nothing new.

Captain Al Haynes and UAL Flight 232 have often been used as the classic CRM case. Haynes used every possible tool available to him after literally losing an engine on his DC10, which caused loss of hydraulics and all flight controls. By using extra flight crew, radio, telephone, and emergency response on the ground, he was able to land his crippled aircraft with many survivors. But he had to go completely outside the box and some of his company's SOPs to accomplish it. There were no checklists or procedures for the situation he found himself in, but the SOP and CRM discipline guided him through the task.

Standard Operating Procedures are the backbone to a safety culture, be it single or multi pilot. Your SOPs spell out your limitations, what you will and will not do. They can be changed or amended as your experience grows, but not during a flight.

SOPs can spell out your weather minimums for a flight. It can be made as detailed as you desire. What minimums for country you know well? What about new country? Remote country? Stable versus unstable weather patterns? How much wind, how much ceiling? How about your currency in particular country?

Another critical SOP, particularly for backcountry flying, is in regard to airstrip operations. For which airstrips are you going to require for yourself an oral briefing first? Or a flight with a more experienced or current pilot? And what specific conditions are you going to require for a particular operation?

Years ago, I performed off-field operations routinely as part of my job. Without large tires or gear. I didn't know about formal SOPs back then, but I still approached every landing with caution and a routine checklist. And decided against very many. These days, for those operations I am usually with a friend who is more current and skilled than I am, and I am very happy to let him go first and evaluate the situation for me. He tells me what he has found and I decide if it meets my SOPs. If not, I wait for him to take off for the next spot.

Earlier I discussed going to a challenging airstrip that a pilot might not be current enough at to have "the razor's edge." Those thought processes are part of an SOP to assure the operation can be conducted safely, with acceptable risk. It is similar to airstrips a pilot has not been to in quite a while, or ever. Decide in advance, in your SOPs, what defines an airstrip you will require an oral or flight check into. And don't let your friends dissuade you. Does it have a reputation for being one of the more challenging strips in the area? All the more reason to pull back and think twice. And remember, it doesn't matter how capable your aircraft is. It matters that you and your aircraft fly as one.

In my country there is one particular airstrip I consider the most difficult, contrary to a lot of popular belief perhaps due to its isolation and lack of use. I used to go into it every year, sometimes quite a few times. But even then, I tried to talk first to the one or two of the other pilots who used it occasionally, to get the latest scoop. Now I might go there once or twice a year, or maybe even every other year. And you can bet my SOP includes talking to the one other pilot I trust regarding not only the surface condition, but the approach and departure. And when I go, I never know for sure if I'm going to land or not until I arrive overhead.

Grow your own safety culture. Your CFI did this for you when you were a student pilot. He listed limitations on your student license and your log book as to where and under what conditions you could solo. New instrument pilots limit their own ceiling and visibility minimums, as do experienced instrument pilots with new aircraft or avionics. Having an autopilot and spelling out how and when you will use it, is an important SOP.

But it is easy for the single pilot, out on his own, to grow away from SOPs and wander alone. And it can become dangerous in a hurry, in just a matter of seconds.

Practice the techniques discussed here! It is

actually better to practice these "Zen" techniques by oneself. Meditation, after all, is done by oneself. The less distractions and outside input, the better. To a point. It is critical, I think, to learn how to meld both inside and outside influences as flying decisions and evaluations are made. It takes constant practice, and no two flights are ever the same.

By keeping yourself aware of what is going on in your mind, and your environment, as you fly, you can maximize your single pilot experience and be just as professional as the best corporate or airline flight crew.

Go out and have some fun while you continue to learn and develop your technique!

The De-Brief

I've had some great de-briefs with flight crews. In the IFR environment, they were often about the approach from 200' to the ground and the nuances of legality, sometimes severe VFR until 200' when you enter the fog. Sometimes these conversations went on for several days, and they were always clarifying, beneficial, and thought-provoking.

I've also had some great de-briefs with myself, while putting the airplane away or driving home afterward. Like most pilots, I have yet to complete the perfect flight, and there is always something to mull over. Sometimes minor, sometimes something bigger. Many times, doing something wrong that I had known better about and forgotten, or ignored. And yes, I have had the occasional sobering de-brief where I have promised myself to NEVER again do what I just got away with. And it is good that those conversations with yourself can haunt you for the rest of your flying career.

De-briefing is a never-ending process that is often more valuable and insightful than the flight itself. It is the single best technique I have found for improving my flying. And it is simple. Maybe not always easy, but simple nonetheless. Just review the flight in your mind from beginning (perhaps the night before) to end (walking away from the airplane). Be critically honest with yourself, not making excuses (explanations, perhaps).

Some really bad flights may stick with you for years, and that is ok. You can't continue to learn from flights that you can't remember, and you must continue to learn.

PHOTO GALLERY

CUB CRAFTERS

TO ORDER: Call 509-248-9491
Monday Through Friday
8 a.m. to 6 p.m.

Prices subject to change

Copper Starter Cable Kit	$ 85.00
Real® Gasket Set for valve rockers	35.60
Felt Baffle Material - 6 ft. roll	12.00
Stainless Steel Push-Pull cables	16.50
Windshields, green or grey	139.00
Clear windshields	119.00
Skylights - green tint	57.50
Side Window Sets (all 6)	
.100 Plexiglass	99.00
.093 Lexan	139.00
Non-Slip Inspection Covers	2.85 ea.
Extra Heavy Duty Mufflers	295.00
Exhaust Stacks- new front & rear	
front standard	315.00
front H.D. reinforced	415.00
rear standard	325.00
rear H.D. reinforced	425.00
Fuel Selector Repair Kit	35.00
Heavy Duty Header Tanks	90.00 ea.
Squared Instrument Panel	250.00
Removeable Rear Seat Crossbar Kit - STC'd	75.00
Plane Booster Wing Tip Kit STC'd with all ribs	675.00
Brake Super Master Cylinders	265.00
Brake Lines for Super Master Cylinders	19.00 ea.
32 gallon fiberglass belly tanks	1595.00
Mr. Funnel - high tech filter	
large	25.00
small	9.95
Extended Baggage Kit	265.00
Rear Seat Storage Kit	125.00
"U" Channel Felt Kit for sliding window	29.00
Floorboards - ½" A/A Marine Plywood w/snug fitting cutouts	
Front	37.50
Rear	37.50
Baggage	20.00
4' Leading Edge Skin Blanks	37.50
Landing Gear Safety Cables	75.00
Inertia Reel Shoulder Harness w/2" lap belt - price per seat	249.00
Aluminum Headliner	200.00
Carb Airbox Repair Kit List $34.10	29.50

Scott 3200 Tailwheel Assembly List $490.00	$ 329.00
8" Tailwheel tires	21.95
8" Tailwheel tubes	7.50
29" Tundra tires	1595.00 pair
26" Tundra tires	1395.00 pair
10" Tundra tailwheel conversion kit	325.00
Fueling Steps - pair	50.00
Heavy Duty Alaska Gear Vees	215.00
Extended Landing Gear - 6"	275.00
3"	275.00
Cabane Vee H.D.	75.00
Shock Struts H.D.	55.00 ea.
1280 H.D. Shock Rings	13.50 ea.
1280 H.D. Cold Weather	16.00 ea.
6" Cleveland Wheel Kit	439.00
Bolt Kits - All bolts, nuts, washers and cotter pins required:	
Wing Attach Kit - both wings	43.25
Tail group attach kit	9.50
Landing gear w/safety cables	37.50
w/out safety cables	36.50
Tailwheel attach kit - 4 spring	12.50
" - 3 spring	12.50
Flap and Aileron Attach Kit	24.50
Tail Surface hinge pin kit	12.50
Tail Surface bushing kit	13.50
4130 Tubing - all sizes - call for pricing	
Steel Weld-On Float Fittings	250.00
Deluxe Seat Sets - wide & soft black or red	375.00
Molded Plastic Rear Seat Stick Cover	75.00
Whelen Strobe System - 3 lights & installation kit	499.00
Heat Robbers	150.00
Defrosters	180.00
Deluxe Door Seals	24.00
Interior Decals	27.50
Super Cub script decals for cowl	11.30
L21 Maintenance Manual	25.00
Lightweight Geared Starters	625.00
"Super Cub - the Airplane" T-shirts	
Adults	9.00
Childrens	7.00
SCPA logo T-shirts and polo shirts	
T-shirts- adult sizes only	9.00
Polo shirts - adult sizes	12.00
Map Pockets	$ 75.00
60 Amp Alternator Conversion Kit - List $588.00	449.00

CALL in your order at 509-248-9491, 8 a.m. to 6 p.m., and we'll send your order out C.O.D. We also accept VISA and MasterCard and personal checks. You can WRITE to us at P.O. Box 9823, Yakima, WA 98909 or STOP BY and see us at 1920 S. 16th Avenue (on the east end of the Yakima Airport) and we will be happy to fill your order.

TOP CUB
STOL System by Cub Crafters, Inc.
NOW AVAILABLE! CALL FOR INFO

SCPA newsletter inserts showing a few of the mods available and popular back in the 1980s.

CUB CRAFTERS SPRING SPECIALS!

INTRODUCING...
STAINLESS STEEL PARTS

Cowl Attach Channels - upper $47.50 ea.
Cowl Attach Channels - lower $47.50 ea.
Tie Down Rings $25.00 ea.
Float Lifting Rings $50.00 pr.

All Stainless Steel with Stainless ¼ turn receptacles

NOTE: The Stainless Steel Lifting Rings attach permanently to your front wing mount bolts and protrude through the wing root fairings.

SPECIAL OFFER
MAP POCKETS

These molded plastic, handy pockets fit between the boot cowl and the front kick panel.

Regular $75.00
NOW $40.95

YOU'VE GOT TO HAVE THEM!
DELUXE SEATS

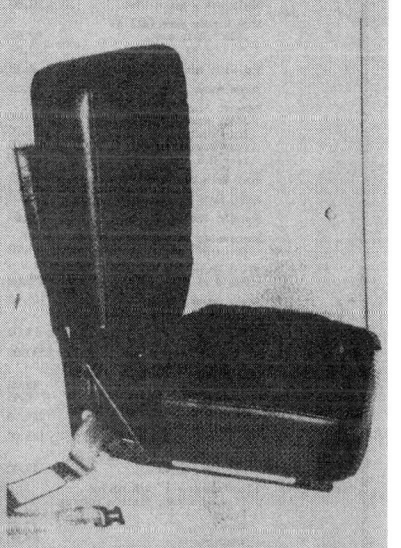

These seats, 3" wider than standard seats, fit like a bucket seat and are made of black SnoSkin vinyl that won't crack even at -50°F. The cloth inserts feel warm in winter and cool in summer. These will extend your range tremendously! Your choice of black or red.

Regular price: $375.00
Sale price: $349.00

The rebuilt and straightened fuselage. About one third of the tubing was replaced, and the turtle deck was added along with other modifications such as the handling tube and float fittings.

Fresh Stits Poly Fiber cover with rib-stitching.

We did away with the ag model swayback and added the turtle deck.

Rear strut reinforcement and the spar cap that is part of the gross weight increase.

The front strut reinforcement, Atley Dodge STC.

Disassembly started. The fabric is off the wing on the right.

The family who works together....Linda, John, Patrick, and Josi strip fabric off the wing.

New leading edges.

Covered in silver, with the new fuel bay for the Atlee Dodge 30-gallon tank. We would have preferred the Dakota 24-gallon tanks, but they were not yet approved for certified Cubs. The Dodge tanks added 11 pounds over stock. Some owners complained about the tanks cracking, but we were meticulous about supporting and angling them correctly and have never had an issue.

Starting the paint scheme outline.

The first, and probably only, certified Cub with carbon fiber side panels. Note the custom leather stick grip. After having one on Harrah's Middle Fork Otter, I had to have another. The circuit breakers were moved to the front panel, but we kept the traditional toggle switches in the right-wing root. With the large fuel tanks, a reliable fuel computer was mandatory.

This is the beautiful hand-made skylight that Wayne King built and molded in his homemade oven. He did the same for his own Cub, and both took several attempts.

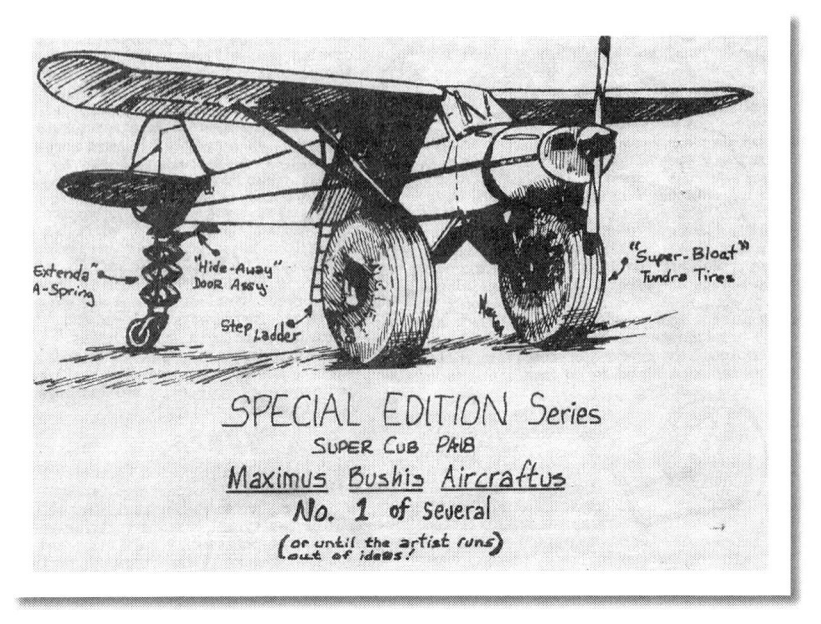

De-Piperizing the Cub

Patrick installing EDO 2000 floats in Alaska.
We had fun with these for four summers.

Still set up for predator control, with respect for the coyote on the side. Note the flagger attached to the left gear leg, and 8:50 tires down to 12 psi. The orange stripes were for visibility, and orange paint on the left-wing strut can be seen in the color photo version.

The original Cub, out in the Owyhees with Bob Hannah, back in the days he actually flew and owned a Super Cub, before "downgrading" to the Scout.

Extreme backcountry flying.
Photo credit: Kasey Lindsay

"The Super Cub is the safest airplane in the world; it can just barely kill you."
—Max Stanley, Northrup Test Pilot

But no one was injured in this accident.

INDEX

INDEX

Amerex	250
AmeriKing	250
Art	68, 70, 75, 167, 179, 181, 251, 253, 255
Attitudes	31, 79, 102, 180, 121, 185, 187
B&C	247
Bayley, Caro	3
BC	237
Black, Bob	Preface
Blackburn, Dwight	202
Borer, Roger	5, 228, 240
Bound For the Backcountry	Forward, 4
Bowers, Peter	148
Brackett	237
Brakes	Preface, 5, 6, 21, 26, 38, 39, 109–111, 169, 197, 233, 239, 249, 264
Bruder, Gerry	79
Bushwheels	233, 236, 239
Carburetor	30
Carrey, Johnny	142
Catto	237
Cavies, George	131
Chamberlain Basin	11, 81
Checklists	93–96, 129, 266
Clark, Alex	245, 247
Cleveland	21, 110, 168, 239, 249

Cold Meadows	25, 26, 55, 56, 59, 129, 135, 137, 138
Combs, Mike	12, 13
Conley, Cort	142
Conway, Carle	77
Cox, Bill	4
CRM	265, 266
Cub Crafters	Forward, 62, 157, 228, 236, 238–240, 242, 249, 250
Dakota	15, 229, 239, 279
Dan's Aircraft	241
Davis, Jerry	52
Davtron	249
De-brief	269
Dodge, Atley	7, 227, 236, 238, 240, 249, 276
Dorris, Bill	56, 138
Drennon, Paul	168
Ego	119, 189, 254, 261
Electronics International (EI)	238
F-22	103
FAA	22, 23, 41–43, 77, 82, 127, 143, 151, 152, 158, 161, 162, 172, 179, 187, 189, 215, 232, 235, 237, 242, 246, 248
Falstead, Hartly	202
Flying B	13, 29

Frye, J.J. — 232
Gaggle — 254, 260, 261
Gann, Ernest — 73
Garmin — 250
Go-arounds — 195, 197–199
Goostrey, John — 41
Grant, Robert S. — 3
Hannah, Bob — 203, 283
Hartzell — 237
Haynes, Al — 266
Hedge, Kerry — 15
Hill, Frank — Preface
Hoem, Sarge — 13
Holm, Richard — Forward, 4
Hoover, Amy — Forward
Hulstrand, Steve — 13
Imeson, Sparky — 105
Jensen — 238
Johnson, Steve — Forward
Johnson, Vaughn — 17
Judgment — 34, 76, 119, 182, 187–193
Keogh, Tim — 209, 242
King — 250
King, Wayne — 229, 241, 245, 281
Knight-Rossiter, Sherry — 191, 199

L-18C .... Forward, 245, 246
Learjets 100, 101, 103
Lindsay, Kasey 284
Low, Dave 155
Lycon 236, 237
Machado, Rod 87
Mackay Bar 81
Madsen, George 109
Mags 39, 40, 66, 95, 96
Markham, Beryl 255
McCarty, Ilona .... Cover
McCauley 5, 236, 237, 248
Microbursts 141, 144
Mountain, Canyon, and Backcountry Flying .... Forward, 27, 68, 91, 169, 194, 207, 213, 216, 255, 257
Navajo 123
Newman, Alex 16
Nippondenso 237
Notes From The Cockpit .... Forward, Preface, 35, 57, 93, 257
Owyhees 283
Pankonin, Steve 17
Piper .... Introduction, 1, 3, 4, 11, 47, 81, 99, 116, 123, 199, 222, 245, 246
Pirsig, Robert 253, 257

Power Curve	105–107, 131, 144, 166, 167
Precise Flight	249
Professional Pilots Inc.	248
Propellers	5, 93, 227, 235–237
Prunty, Tom	75, 76, 79
Quality	20, 187, 234, 254
Richmond, Jim	Forward, 7, 11, 24, 228
Robinson, John	99
Rogers, John	229
Rogers, Will	177
Root Ranch	11, 15, 17, 26
Rosen	228, 241
Running Creek	109, 110
Rusk, Bill	232
SCPA	Forward, Introduction, 9, 11, 19, 23, 26, 217, 218, 261, 272
Selway Lodge	33, 35
Sensenich	5, 235–237
Senses	192, 260, 264, 265
Sheldon, Don	3
Simplot	141, 142, 144, 258
Skis	27, 95, 129, 130, 135–139, 240
Skunberg, Lenny	Cover, Preface, 111, 255
SkyTech	237
Smith Bros.	229

Stanley, Max … 3, 285
Steve's Aircraft (Steve's) … 238, 248
Stitts … 240
Stockhill, Mike … 77
STOL … Forward, Introduction, 12, 69, 82, 86 101, 105, 227, 253, 258
Stowell, Rich … 163
Sulphur Creek … 261, 263
Supercub.org … Forward, 232, 245
Survival … 29, 55–57, 59–62, 64, 67, 73, 131, 135, 136, 152, 154, 188
Taylor, Gordon & Clarence … 3
Terry, Hal … 155
The Joy of Soaring … 77
Thrustline … 237, 248
Tubbs, Steve … 229, 245
Twain, Mark … 45
Twin Otter … 82, 84, 120, 166, 207, 258
Virag, Irene … 253
Williams, Ed … Forward
Williams, Patrick … 242, 245, 277, 282, Back Cover
Wipaire … 240
Woodhouse, Bob … 16, 17
Yeager, Chuck … 75
Zen … 251, 253, 269

INDEX

Made in the USA
Columbia, SC
06 June 2025